A Decade of Fear

Norma McCluskie

A DECADE OF FEAR

ISBN: 978-0-557-44970-5

Published and Printed by Lulu.com
http://www.lulu.com/product/11183757

Edited and Designed by Chris O'Byrne
www.editingyourworld.com

DEDICATION

This is a story that needed to be told.

To my husband Bernard, the love of my life that inspired me to write this book....

My pride and joy are my children, my three daughters, Donna, Patricia and Diane, also my three sons, Martin, Sean and James. I praise them for their sincerity and commend them for the goals they set for themselves to make all their fantasies come true. I believe their dreams surpassed all my expectations.

I appreciate my sons and daughters in law, John, Robert, and Patrick; Leslie, Kerry and Olga... They know the true meaning of family.

I pray for my grandchildren, my great-grandchildren, may their lives be secure, happy and full of love... I have so much hope and well wishes for all of them.

This dedication is especially for our mothers and fathers who left this world before us, but were the backbone of our resilience, our integrity and dedication to family.

For my friend, Delise, who steered me in the right direction.

To Colleen, who helped me immensely.

This is a tribute to my son Sean, who took the time to read my book endless times and corrected my mistakes. His confidence in my book was resolute.

To all the friends and relatives that stood at our side at our time of sorrow.

To my beloved son, Benny, who did not have the chance to live his life, but has been an inspiration for all of us.

And an angel came....

SOURCES OF INFORMATION

My Own Recollections

My Husband's Recollections

My Daughters' Recollections

Public Information from the Internet

Stories from the Chicago Tribune and Chicago Sun

Captive City—some inserts that are common knowledge

Chicago State's Attorney's Office

Public Information in Chicago's Archives

"Trail of Memories", written in 1945, Trail, BC, Canada

TABLE OF CONTENTS

INTRODUCTION

This is a true story about a young couple who owned and operated a small tavern in the city of Chicago. Norma came from a small city in British Columbia, Canada. Ben came from a small town in Scotland, United Kingdom. Both grew up in these small towns where everything was innocent. They came from loving families who encouraged them to be independent.

After the Second World War, many Europeans searched for a better life. Ben remembered the war when all of his four brothers were in the service and away for several years. His parents doted on him, but after the conflict was over, employment in Scotland was scarce. He decided to follow one of his brothers who immigrated to Canada. For many from Europe, Canada was a stepping stone to the United States.

They met and married in Toronto, Ontario, Canada but decided that Chicago offered more opportunities for them. I remember how naive we were and the big city was both exciting and scary.

With partners, they purchased a small tavern on the north side of Chicago. This was their first venture into a business that promised great rewards. They were excited at the prospects, but never being in a business before, found there were many drawbacks.

They hired a bartender for Friday nights, just for a couple of hours each week. The bartender was a hitman, although it was some time before they became aware of his true profession.

The holdup was the turning point in their relationship. Their partners decided the pub was not for them.

This is a story of the many events that this couple endured. It is also a story about survival.

This book took many years to write. Norma said, "I needed to dig into my past to remember all the details and incidents that made me a person. I remembered all the wonderful experiences I had of growing up with my family who loved me. I also recalled my yearning for adventure, which eventually brought me to Chicago."

Chicago in the 1950s and the 1960s was a city riddled with crime. It was also a city where organized crime flourished. The police departments turned a blind eye and their attention elsewhere when many of these transgressions were committed. Many officers were on the take and bribery was a fact of life.

Sam DeStefano was an unscrupulous character. He was a loan shark and a big time hoodlum, who the police knew well. He operated a lucrative business loaning monies to many crooks, but also to politicians, judges and attorneys. He had them in his pocket.

Sam was also a sadist, a devil worshiper, and a murderer. He was a man with no conscience. He was a rapist and a criminal and it is documented that he was one of the worst torturers in the history of the United States. He was evil.

In order to collect these loans, he hired hitmen such as Charles Crimaldi who used forceful tactics. Guns and baseball bats were the weapons of choice. Chuck was as brutal as Sam. He enjoyed putting fear in a man or would murder him for a few bucks and the thrill.

We hired Chuck as our bartender, but after the holdup, the events that happened were unpredictable and intimidating. He was the ultimate bartender, he had charisma, personality and he was deadly.

There was no law for protection. We were a pawn for the State's Attorney who put their interests before people in order to pursue bigger political gains.

After the death of our son, we fought for our sanity. There were

2

no answers and to depend on the authorities was a joke. In Chicago, there was no justice.

This is a story that is both heart-warming and heart-wrenching. It is written in my own words and the incidents are truthfully described as I remembered them. The conversations are as close as I can recall. Each word may not be the exact word or phrase used, but the story is true.

This is a story about torture, murder, bribery and hate. It shows the lengths a mobster or the State's Attorney will go to for their own gain.

It is also a story about love and family. It is about caring for each other and the many friends who cared about us.

These are my recollections and the names of persons used are also real people.

This is my story of ten years in our lifetime that we called a "Decade of Fear."

I dedicate this book to my children, my grandchildren and my great-grandchildren. I also dedicate this book to my beautiful son who lost his life when he was five years old. Without our love and a quest for justice for him, this book would not be possible. He lives in my heart and not a day goes by that I do not think about him. He is our guardian angel.

Norma McCluskie

Norma McCluskie

PROLOGUE

I like to sit by myself at his gravesite. The guards are gone. It is peaceful and I can lose myself in my thoughts. What if? It is quiet, I can hear the birds chirping in the background, but I block all the sounds out and I can only feel my heart beating. I am sad. I think of what could have been. What if we had done things differently that awful night? We cannot blame each other. Ben says, "I should have taken them out together." I say to myself, "You're a coward. You stood there, afraid to move. You depended on him to save our children." But I tell myself, "We had never been in this kind of situation, a fire, we didn't know the smoke would come so quickly." Ben forgot where the bunk beds were since we had just purchased them. He said, "I was groping in the dark, I could not find them." It is easy to place the blame on one another, but we know we have to stand together; it was out of our hands. There was a hand greater than ours that reached out for our little boy and took him from us. I can see him among the angels; he is happy as he looks down on us and wonders why we are so sad. And an angel came.

Norma McCluskie

CHAPTER 1: THE HOLDUP

October 5, 1962, was a Friday like so many other Fridays. When I woke up, the darkness was still upon us. It was early, but there was so much to do. My day began as usual. The floor had to be swept and washed. The bar had to be cleaned from the night before and lunches prepared for our clientele. Ben was up early and filled some coolers with beer for me. He checked the liquor bottles making sure they were adequate so everything would be easier when the men came in. At 6:30 AM he left for his construction job.

As he was leaving he said, "This job is closer to home, I don't need to travel far. I should be home in the afternoon. Besides, the job is nearly finished; the brickwork is almost done. It is only going to last for a few more days."

I was grateful for that; it was nice when he came home earlier. He could see the kids before bedtime, but also the day would not seem so long for me.

I smiled at him and said, "You must be tired." I had been asleep when he had come to bed after closing the pub at 2:00 AM The hours were long and demanding.

He smiled back. "Will be home early today," he responded and waved his hand as he left.

At 7:00 AM I was ready to open the pub. My usual morning clientele was standing outside quite impatiently. They were peering and banging on the window. I gave them a wave as I glanced at the clock and at the dot of 7:00 AM, pushed the buzzer under the counter, unlocking the door. The men piled into the pub, pushing and shoving to be served first.

"Come on, guys," I shouted cheerfully, "I will get to all of you." Work for the men started at 7:30 AM. They had only thirty minutes for quick refreshment and to get to their jobs. There was often a full bar and the men joked around with each other. They knew each other well, a number of them having worked together for many years. They were mischievous and full of pranks that they played on each other. Everyone enjoyed a good laugh. Most worked across the street at Cribben and Sexton stove factory. At 11:30 AM they would return for lunch.

These mornings with the men were enjoyable. They were fun and respectful. After a few quick drinks, they rushed to their jobs, looking forward to their next break. A few would purchase a miniature bottle of spirits to carry back to their work hidden in their pockets. I remembered how hard my father worked and knew these men were trying to earn an honest living.

As I tidied up the bar, thoughts of my father filled my mind. An immigrant like many of my customers, he had immigrated to Canada as a young man of sixteen. Being the oldest son of a family of thirteen, where only eleven had survived, he had never met many of his siblings.

He had worked in Montreal for a time before going to the city of Trail in British Columbia, Canada, where I and my brothers and sister were born. My father decided to work in the smelter, a processing plant, and he did so for thirty-five years. Because he had no education, he often said it was the perfect job for him, but my memory was about how hard he worked in a dirty and thankless job so he could give us a better life. He had come through the Depression as so many men had and was grateful for a job.

After the last customer left, I locked the tavern door to take my girls to school at 8:00 AM.

"Come on," I said, "we are running late." After dropping the girls off at school, we returned to the tavern. I fixed breakfast for our boys and then took them upstairs to the apartment before reopening the pub.

Used glasses were still sitting on the counter and tables. I washed them quickly and put them back in order. My attention turned to the kitchen where there was still preparation to be done for the lunches. I glanced at the clock. Ret would be here soon. When she arrived, I would begin my usual Friday routine and take the checks we had cashed through the week to the bank. These were usually company checks. The bank would exchange them for money so we could have the funds available to cash our customer's checks. Friday was payday.

As I worked tirelessly, my thoughts returned to our partner, Ret. I had seen her and her husband Packy a few times at social events, but did not know them well. They also came from Scotland as my husband Ben did. They had much in common. I remember when we met through our husbands when we were contemplating the purchase of the pub. The four of us had spent the evening together discussing our options and could not conceal our excitement. This business was a first for all of us.

Henrietta Burns, nicknamed Ret, was taller than me, blond and blue-eyed, not slim, but medium in size. She was attractive and had a personality similar to Ben's. They both liked attention, loved people and a social life. Her husband Patrick, who earned the nickname Packy, was very different than his wife and I often wondered what they had in common. Packy was a very reserved and private individual. His face was ominous, never showing any emotion, and he rarely smiled. He appeared cold and aloof, but he and Ben got along very well. I shrugged my shoulders and returned to the task at hand.

My thoughts were interrupted as I glanced up and Ret entered the premises with her youngest daughter. We exchanged greetings. I said, "I am out of here, will be back as soon as I can. I have already begun the lunches, maybe you can finish up. The boys are upstairs."

When I got into my car, I noticed the red car parked across the street. It was a bright, new car and that caught my eye. New cars were rarely seen in our neighborhood. I shrugged off my observation and got into my car.

I spoke out loud to myself, "Wonder who that car belongs to? I have never seen it before." I made a mental note to ask Ret if she knew whose car it was. I was not aware that someone in the red car was watching me. I also did not notice that a car was following me. Usually I was very observant of my surroundings, but not this particular morning. Later I questioned myself. I decided my lack of observation was due to my continued routine every Friday. I never expected anything to be different.

The bank was only a few miles away along Chicago Avenue. It was a route I had taken many times. I took care of our business at the bank, then proceeded back to the tavern, hurrying along. My thoughts went over each chore that had to be accomplished before lunchtime. My hair was still in curlers and I needed to change my clothes. I glanced at the clock on the dashboard. The time was close to 11:00 AM.

Even though the bar was open, we usually did not see customers until 11:30 AM. I ran upstairs to check on the younger children. My next step was to check out the bar to be certain everything was in order and ready for lunch. Because the bar was usually three deep, there would be standing room only. Most men wanted to have more than one drink and demanded to be served quickly. Anticipating these orders, I usually poured several shot glasses of whiskey in advance and stood them in a row to save time. By knowing what the customer drank, we could grab a whiskey quickly and keep them content.

Ret was putting the finishing touches on the lunches. We joked around for a bit, and then we heard the door open. I was standing at the edge of the table and could see the length of the bar, therefore

I was the first to see the two men with black ski masks and guns coming towards the kitchen.

I whispered in a quiet voice, "I think we are going to be held up." I did not panic but with a swift motion tossed the bag of money under the table leaving the moneybox that contained about eleven hundred dollars and change.

Ret laughed and thought I was kidding. However, as they stood in the open doorway, her expression changed as she realized this was not the case. They did not speak, but waved their guns in the air. Ret backed up against the sink and I backed up against the door to the apartment. Fear gripped my heart for the children who were upstairs. The men rambled through the kitchen, throwing open drawers and cupboards and as they did so, I slipped into the bar. I knew the gun was under the counter. Having never fired a gun, I thought I might brandish the firearm and say, "Drop it." My hands were shaking as I picked up the revolver. I thought this would scare them. It seemed an eternity, but several minutes later they came out of the kitchen. They only had the box; they had not found the rest of the money. I could not speak, my voice had disappeared.

Once I started firing the gun, I couldn't stop. They were firing back at me and the noise was deafening. As I stand less than five-feet tall, I just ducked behind the counter. I fired all of the bullets that were in the chamber, striking the ceiling and the jukebox and one bullet struck one of the robbers.

He screamed. "I've been hit!" I felt myself flinch. I could not believe I had shot someone.

The newspapers said someone threw a stool at me, but that was not true. It was like something one would see in a movie in slow motion. It seemed so unreal. As they exited the bar, money was flying everywhere. The robbers jumped into a waiting getaway car and I heard the car speed from the scene. It suddenly became quiet, except for the screeching tires as they fled. Believing it was safe, I crawled along the floor behind the bar and reached for the phone and called 911. Ret came out of the kitchen to see if I was all right. She asked me in a shaky, low voice, almost a whisper. "Are you okay?" She peered around the corner, and looked at me with the gun in my hand. In a shrill and excited voice she shrieked, "My God, Norma, are you crazy? What is wrong with you? Are you mad? What made you do that? When I heard the gunfire, I was scared to death. I was afraid to come out here."

When I stood up, my knees were trembling, I responded, "You know, Ret, I didn't even think about it. I just did it. God knows I know nothing about guns. I scared myself." We hugged each other; laughing nervously, both of us traumatized by the events and happy to be alive.

The police arrived at the same time as the customers. Seeing them on the premises, our customers wanted to know what was going on. The officers took their time and alleged they did not receive the correct address. They had gone south instead of north on Albany Avenue. I let Ret give some of the testimony, while I ran upstairs to make sure the children were not harmed. I walked towards the bedroom and opened the door quietly, my heart pounding. What made me think one of the bullets could reach this far? I was thankful Marty was still sleeping. Benny and Ret's daughter, Janine, was in the kitchen playing with toys, not aware anything was wrong. Ret and I went outside to retrieve what was left of the money they had dropped in their flight. The customers joined in to help.

The officers retrieved casings from the bullets and noticed blood by the door that indicated one of the alleged robbers had been hit.

It was exciting and frightening at the same time. Reporters came from several newspapers, making a big deal of the story and asking us to pose for pictures. They wanted a full story and description of how the robbery went down. Our clientele also wanting to know every detail and we were trying to oblige them.

At first we felt like celebrities, but soon it became annoying.

Everyone was chatting at the same time. The jukebox was a mess, plus the customers were examining the premises for bullet holes. I could not wait for the lunch hour to end as the questions were endless. They were beginning to irk me as we were asked to repeatedly give an account of the robbery. The pub was full of excitement as we tried to serve food and drinks. Neither we, nor the customers, had ever experienced a holdup. Once the lunch hour was over, we took a breath, but realized we still had the police to contend with.

The police's excuse that they received the wrong address really bothered me. Although I was excited when calling 911, I was confident they received the correct address. Ben and Packy were working down the street not far from the tavern. They heard the news, I believe from a reporter.

Ben said, "My wife did well, I don't need to come home." He smiled, turned to the men on the job and explained what happened.

Most customers had left to go back to their jobs. The reporters from the media came and went, but the officers who had been on the premises for some time were everywhere searching for clues. We were nervous. A ton of questions were fired at us from the two policemen, but the robbers were masked and it happened so fast.

I watched as they dusted the kitchen for fingerprints. I explained to the officers that the suspects were wearing gloves but had noticed that they had dark eyes. I thought they were either Italian or Puerto Rican. They nodded their heads and wrote everything down. We tried to resume business as usual, but it was a very upside down day as we relived the events repetitively.

One officer asked, "Where did you get your gun?"

"We bought it from an ex-police officer," I said, and gave his name. They did not respond, looked at each other and let the subject drop.

After the officers left, the place was quiet. Ret and I cleaned the bar. Lost in thought, we worked together in silence. We then sat down to discuss all that had transpired.

I was first to speak, "This wouldn't have happened if we still had Duke." It reminded both of us of how much we had depended on him. Ret looked at me in agreement, nodding her head, both of us realizing we could have been hurt. A worse thought was that one of us could have been killed.

Tavern Owner's Wife Fires, Routs Bandits

The doughty wife of a tavern owner slipped out of the sight of two bandits yesterday in the tavern, found a revolver behind the bar and, tho she had never fired a revolver before, routed them with a fusillade.

Mrs. Norma McCluskie, 29, who lives above the tavern operated by her husband, Ben, at 718 N. Albany av., told police she believed she wounded at least one of the men.

Police were inclined to agree with her. They found blood on the floor of the tavern and blood in the stolen car abandoned by the bandits. They also found $400 dropped outside the tavern by the two, who got away with $1,100.

Hurls Money Under Table

Just before the holdup Mrs. McCluskie returned to the tavern with $2,000 from a bank. The money was to be used for cashing checks. When she saw the men enter the tavern, she threw it under a kitchen table, among pots and pans, where the robbers failed to find it.

She told Police Sgt. George Robinson that when she got back to the tavern with the $2,000 she went directly to the kitchen where Mrs. Henrietta Burns, 27, of 542 N. Kedzie av., was at work. Thru the open door she saw two men enter the tavern and walk toward the kitchen.

"They look like holdup men," she told Mrs. Burns. Then she took the $2,000 from a money bag and threw it among the pots and pans. Mrs. Burns hid a metal cash box, which contained $200 in coins and $1,200 in bills, between a stove and table.

Mrs. Norma McCluskie holds revolver she fired at robbers.

Bandits Cover Faces

"We know you've got the money. Where is it?" said the two gunmen, who wore handkerchief masks and gloves. They shoved Mrs. Burns around while Mrs. McCluskie, unnoticed, slipped from the kitchen into the barroom. There she got the gun and waited for the men to leave the kitchen.

Her first shot hit the wall, she said. One of the men threw a bar stool at her. The other one shot at her. As they ran out she fired four more shots.

"I put one in the ceiling, one in the juke box, and one in one of the men. I don't know where the other one hit," she said.

Leave Cash Box in Lot

After dropping the coins and the 200 $1 bills, the bandits threw the metal cash box in a vacant lot and drove away. Policemen Michael Lazzaro and John Brusich said the two bandits were seen changing cars at Homan avenue and Ohio street. The car they used for the holdup was stolen from a parking lot at 2355 Ohio st.

Mrs. McCluskie, mother of four children, 1 to 6 years old, called her husband after the holdup.

"You did all right. There's no need for me to come home from work," he told her.

15

CHAPTER 2: DUKE

We sat quietly and my thoughts were on Duke. How I came to love him. After we purchased the tavern from Bernice and Ed, Bernice said to us, "One thing I have to mention is the dog. His name is Duke and I need to leave him here. It is the only home he has ever had. Ed says we need to put him down. I was hoping if you decide to buy the place, you would keep him." She had tears in her eyes as she put her hand on the dog's neck and scratched him with affection. The dog licked her hand, returning the warmth.

"Ed won't let me take him to the resort we bought." Her face was strained as she looked at us with hope. We looked at the dog, a large Doberman pinscher that did not appear too friendly.

I thought, *We had not bargained for a dog, and he does look mean.* I had a dog while growing up and was hesitant about becoming attached to another one.

Ben quickly said, "Sure, we'll keep him. We need a good watchdog."

Later I questioned, "Are you sure we want to keep that dog? How is he going to react to the kids? All the dog knows is this pub. You know what they say about these dogs, they can turn on you."

Ben replied, "He will be all right. He's old, Norma, and he is not going to hurt anyone. You don't want the woman to put him down, do you?" I shook my head no. Ben liked dogs. We kept the dog.

Duke became my dog; he was my companion and loved

the children. They gave him a lot of attention, which he enjoyed. He wore a muzzle when he went outdoors to protect outsiders. Duke disliked uniforms and also wore the muzzle whenever the postman, a policeman, a deliveryman or anyone in uniform entered the premises. While we cashed checks, he sat without his muzzle inside the doorway leading upstairs. He deterred anyone from entering beyond the door and would let out a low growl to voice his disapproval. No one had the courage to venture past the entrance. He was a wonderful watchdog. At night he roamed the premises and nobody dared to enter.

CHAPTER 3: CONFLICT

We were grateful the robbery did not happen on a weekend or a holiday when all the children were upstairs in the apartment. On those days, it was always pretty hectic. The older kids teased the younger children and someone was always running up and down the stairs. Any one of the children could have come downstairs and walked into danger. It was a sobering thought.

Soon afterwards, we found out that the robbers had been arrested only a few blocks away from the tavern. Apparently, after leaving the crime scene, they raced through a red light and were stopped by the police. Because they were known criminals and acting suspicious, the men were brought to the police station for questioning. Fingerprints and mug shots were taken, but the men were later released. The suspect who had been shot went undetected by the police. I was concerned that I may have killed someone.

Later, in a police report, the officers claimed the robbers were seen changing cars at Homan Avenue and Ohio Street. They alleged the car used in the holdup was stolen from a parking lot at 3355 Ohio Street.

Being enthusiastic about our business, danger had never crossed our minds. My attention once again returned to our children. There were a total of eight kids, we each had four. We would be devastated if anything happened to any of them.

We had purchased the tavern in May 1960 and by the end of the summer of 1961 it had become evident that Packy was no longer happy with the arrangement. He felt he was working hard as a bricklayer and Ben had it easier running the pub. Ben offered to change positions.

"I miss working," Ben said, "but Packy doesn't want to work the pub. The only solution I can see is that we both work and you girls will have to take care of the pub. This worries me because I do not like to see you girls here on your own. Perhaps we can hire someone."

"It defeats the purpose, Ben. We can manage. We know most of the customers," I responded.

"I know, but you have a new baby to take care of. And there should be a man around."

"I know, but Ret and I will be okay. We have Duke and he won't let anything happen to us. I think we can handle things and if not, we will have to try something else."

Ben's approach to the business was second to none, his easygoing manner and enthusiasm encouraged customers to frequent the pub and they felt at home. He humored the men and entertained the ladies. Packy was quiet and reserved and was not as sociable. He was tired after a days work and this possibly was the reason for his resentment.

I was not sure we could handle the bar with the same ease as Ben, but I knew we would be efficient. Mornings and afternoons were quieter. Lunch would be our busiest and most challenging time. At night, the men would take over. Weeknights, Packy wanted to close early. Ben was not in favor of this. Packy only worked every other night and Ben did not see this as a hardship.

Ben said, "If we are not consistent in our hours people will stop coming to the pub. They will go to other ones in the area. We need to stay open the same hours, even if some nights are quiet. Look Packy, if you want to leave early, I will close the pub."

It had been easier when Ben worked with us. There was more

time to take care of our children and do the cleaning. When he returned to work, everything became difficult. We could not keep up with the chores. Ret no longer could leave early. Our time was split between waiting on customers and slipping into the kitchen to try and get a head start for the next day. It was hectic. Lunches needed to be prepared in advance. Subsequently, both of us could be available to serve the bar; we tried to reorganize the kitchen to be more efficient. The hours were long and tempers were short. Now we had a new problem to contend with, a holdup. I shivered at the thought.

The holdup weighed heavy on my mind. We were two women alone, which was not a good thing. When we had Duke we felt safe, but Duke was gone. He had been killed by a bus and left in an alley to die. When he did not come home for several days, we hunted all over the neighborhood. Finally, a policeman gave us the sad news. The level of safety we felt with Duke was gone and we were vulnerable.

CHAPTER 4: HAPPIER TIMES

I thought back to the beginning and remembered when we discovered the bar. Ben mentioned that a bricklayer friend and he were discussing going into business. He wanted to show me the pub they had in mind.

"What do you think?" He was excited and energized as he showed me the tavern. "This would be another income for us and we would not have to worry about the winters. You know how hard it is to get work in the winter. We will need a couple of thousand dollars to get started."

I was impressed and a little excited at the prospect of being in business. I did not know anything about pubs, but liked the idea.

When we drove past the tavern, there were cars parked everywhere and the pub appeared busy. I said wispily and a little disappointed, "It is a pretty grimy neighborhood. There are a lot of factories, which is probably why it is so dirty, but I guess that's supposed to be a good thing." I added, "It's not a very good area to raise the kids; what are your thoughts?"

He replied and seemed agitated, "The kids will be fine. I have seen worse places in Scotland." I did not respond. Ben did not like to be challenged. I had seen worse places as well, but I was not sure if it was a place I wanted to bring up my kids.

Weeds were growing everywhere. One could hardly see the sidewalk. The factory windows were dirty. The building needed painting. Papers were left on the street and the breeze was blowing them around. No one made an effort to pick them up. Men in overalls were walking around and greeting each other. Some were going into the factory, while others were leaving.

Ben remarked, "They work in shifts." We drove around the block several times. We noticed scores of people and activity in the area. The adults were conversing, while plenty of children played in front of their homes. It looked like a happy community.

We found a Catholic school and church located on Fulton Street just south of Albany Avenue. Saint Mathews consisted of several large grey buildings; but the outside looked old and in need of repair.

"Look," I said, "a Catholic church, stop so we can see the inside, it looks pretty old."

Ben stopped the car and we got out and went into the church. The church was small, but the interior was wonderful. Its theme was angels and they were painted above the altar in bright, beautiful, soft colors. Next to the church and school was a convent.

"Let's knock on the door and ask if we can see the school, what do you think?"

Ben replied, "That's a good idea."

A tiny nun came to the door and smiled at us warmly. We smiled back and asked, "Is it possible we can see the school? We are planning on moving into the area and have children that are school age."

"Yes, of course," she replied, and walked us to the little schoolhouse. The classrooms were full of color and imagination. We were thrilled. I could not wait to tell Ret, as she was concerned if there was a Catholic school and church in the neighborhood.

We thanked Sister Teresa, the tiny lady with a huge smile. She introduced us to other nuns in the convent. They were extraordinary people and as we spoke to them, we knew their energy and enthusiasm would reflect on the children. Their optimistic outlook would encourage our kids to have a positive outlook on life.

CHAPTER 5: ALBANY AVEVUE

It was a small tavern located on the northwest side of Chicago Avenue at 718 N Albany Avenue, a small side street situated just west of the viaduct. The street could easily be missed if one drove by too quickly. The pub was a two-story building south of Chicago Avenue and east of Laramie Street, nestled in a large factory area. A smaller factory sat at the base of the street. As one turned off Chicago Avenue, going around the bend onto Albany Avenue, the pub was located in the center of the block. An empty lot was situated on one side of the building and a small house on the other side that sat further back from the street.

Factories were everywhere. Cribben and Sexton was the largest, a stove factory directly across the avenue from the pub. This factory covered the entire block. Also in the vicinity were Kraft Foods, the railway and many smaller factories. At the end of the street on the corner was another pub called The 700 Club, where two men rented the premises and the owners lived upstairs. There were a total of five pubs in the area. The factories employed so many people that every tavern had their share of business. The proprietors from all of the pubs were friendly with each other. Ben was afraid someone would purchase the pub before we made a decision.

"Pubs don't sell that fast, it has been on the market for a while," I said, "We need to think about everything before we make a decision. First, we need to get our finances in order. You need to be patient."

I liked the little pub with its sixteen stools and several tables in the center of the room. There was one step to the entrance door of the tavern, which was situated in the middle of the building. Glass blocks were inserted for windows on each side of the doorway. They jutted out like bay windows, allowing only a trickle of light into the pub. To the left of the foyer, just inside the pub, there was a jukebox that sat under one of the windows. Situated to the right of the entry was a payphone and cigarette machine. Another door was next to the phone that led to the apartment upstairs, which was locked from the inside and seldom used. An entrance at the foot of the stairs from the apartment led outside, this door was adjacent to the pub entrance.

The pub had a dropped ceiling made of heavy canvas material in a deep maroon color that covered most of the windows on the left side of the room. As only half of the windows were visible, very little light came into the area. The tiled floor was slightly worn. A large air conditioner sat at the rear of the pub to the left against the back wall. Behind the wall was a tiny kitchen; the stairs to the right led to the apartment above. A back door opened into the fenced yard. At the end of the lot sat a garage that was never used for a car. It would eventually become a playhouse for the children.

NEIGHBORHOOD CHILDREN, ALBANY AVENUE

DONNA, PATRICIA, BENNY, MARTIN

The bar itself was not large, but compact. Entering the pub from the doorway, it was easy to see the sixteen stools wound around the bar in a line on the right hand side. The seats were small, but comfortable, with no backs so one could swivel around. In the middle of the bar on the back wall was the cash register, behind it were mirrors with shelves on both sides. Bottles of liquor organized into the order of their popularity sat on the shelves. The beer glasses below the liquor bottles were placed on white towels, the shot glasses next to them. They glistened under the small lights from the ceiling. The sink and washing facilities along with the ice machine and coolers were under the counter with the barrels of beer. Shiny taps were located on the top of the bar used to pour the draft beer.

There was a door at the end of the bar that led to a damp and musty basement. We were not aware that the basement flooded from time to time. Beside this entry was the pub telephone. At the end of the bar on the far side towards the kitchen was another cooler against the wall used for carryouts, usually six-packs of beer. Next to this cooler was a half door to deter persons from coming behind the bar.

The restrooms were located at the back, just before the entrance to the kitchen. The lady's bathroom was located in front of another half door to the kitchen. It was relatively clean. The men's lavatory was on the outside wall and was dirty and smelled of urine. One could see on the walls where men had missed the target.

The half door to the kitchen also served as a counter. It was kept bolted from the inside while serving food and cashing checks. Duke sat just inside the door to the right at the entranceway going upstairs.

Ben and I drove around the area several times in the weeks that followed. We entered the pub more than once. Ed and Bernice were only too happy to accommodate us. It was a very busy bar. The owners had allowed us to try our hand at pulling a few pints of beer.

"What's your name?" a customer asked me, smiling. I looked

up at him. His voice was pleasant, but his face was old and worn. I noticed some of his teeth were missing.

I smiled at him. "Norma."

"That's a nice name. The boys and I will see that you're all right."

CHAPTER 6: OUR BARTENDER

Chuck, our Friday night bartender, came to work just before 8 PM. There was a buzz in the bar and everyone was still talking about the robbery.

Chuck asked, "What's going on?"

Ben responded, "The girls were robbed at gunpoint this morning and the robbers got away with a lot of cash."

I glanced at Chuck. For some reason his facial expressions caused me to ask without hesitation in a slightly agitated voice, "They got away. Do you know anything about this?"

Chuck stared at me. "No, no," he replied, with a startled look on his face.

Ben glared at me as if I had stepped out of line, motioning for me to be quiet. Chuck seemed surprised that we had a holdup. His body language indicated that he felt uneasy.

Staring at us, he said, "I hope you don't think I had something to do with this?" He paused, "God, Ben, you know me better than that." He appeared offended.

Ben said, "Of course not, but we need to explore every avenue to see if we can find out who robbed us. It was a lot of money to lose and we need to ask questions. Someone knew our schedule and knew these girls were alone. Many bars do the same thing we do, but they were not robbed, we were. We need to think about this because there are kids here. It worries us."

Chuck responded with compassion, "I understand, Ben. I am sorry about the robbery."

Previously, Ben, Packy and I had discussed the possibility that Chuck somehow was involved in the holdup or knew something about it.

Ben said, "What do you think? Chuck knows a lot of undesirables; do you believe he would set us up?"

I replied, "I hope not. You know him better than any of us. Do you think he would do something like that?"

Packy indicated he was not sure. He was a person who liked to mull a situation over and think seriously about it. The conversation had given us food for thought. I asked the question that was on our minds. Chuck's behavior suggested that I had insulted him. Ben was annoyed at my audacity. Packy did not express an opinion and kept silent. For me, it had been a long day and I was not sure if I believed him or not.

Chuck said, "Look, I know a lot of people in this neighborhood and I will put some feelers out and see what I can find out." We left it at that.

Later after closing the pub, Ben scolded me, "Norma, you can't go around accusing people if you have no proof. Chuck was offended. I know we discussed the possibility earlier, but if you were patient he might have given his hand away." He paused and then said, "If he was involved we will never know, he just put his guard up."

Feeling betrayed, I replied, "I don't care. Sometimes he acts strange, and he always has some weird characters hanging around him." I added, "You know, I thought they were Italian and Chuck is Italian."

He put his arm around me, laughing and speaking softly, "So are you. I know you have had a rough day. I thought you were pretty brave." I got his point.

30

CHAPTER 7: SUSPECTS

We were not deterred by the robbery, but were anxious. We realized there were negative aspects to every business. We began taking precautions in the way we did business, switching around our banking hours and making more use of the buzzer on the tavern door. The purpose was to screen the people who came through it. Ben had a steel bar put across the inside of the front of the door so that when we were closed no one could get the door open, even if it were unlocked. Business continued as usual and we were pleased when the conversations changed to a lighter subject.

Several weeks later, two detectives came to see Ret and I with photographs in their hands. They asked if we could identify anyone in the pictures.

I studied them, shook my head and said, "Their faces were covered with masks; I could not identify them."

Ret, however, lifted one of the photos into her hands, examined it carefully and explained in an excited voice, "This is the man who was sitting at the bar the morning of the holdup."

This had taken place while I was at the bank. Ret showed them exactly where he sat, gave them a description of his clothing and what he ordered to drink.

"We never have any customers at that time. He was the only person at the bar, that's why I remember him," she exclaimed.

The officers were as excited as we were. "Are you sure?"

Ret said, "Oh yes, I am very sure." She was pleased with herself and excited that she could identify one of the robbers.

The detectives explained that the men were photographed the morning of the robbery. They were stopped for a traffic violation. Because they were known criminals and acting suspiciously, they were taken to the police station, questioned and had their pictures taken. Their names were Frank Santucci, Anthony Donato and Robert Chesser.

Chuck was aware that the authorities had photos of the three men alleged to be the robbery suspects. He knew Ret had identified one of them, but did not say much. We told him the names of the suspects, but there was not any indication as to whether he knew them or not. He nodded his head and did not say anything that would have aroused our suspicion. He suddenly adopted a nervous twitch while he darted around behind the bar, trying to avoid any conversation with us. He had many faces and I began to think he also had many personalities. However, the expression in his eyes always gave him away. He was not a good liar.

When I think back, I remember he became very quiet. Everyone in the pub was talking about the robbery, but Chuck kept a low profile. He did not make any comments.

I said to him, "Isn't it great that Ret has such a good memory to identify that guy? Otherwise they would have gotten away. Aren't you glad they are caught?"

He smiled and said, "Yeah, sure." I looked at him and realized his smile was not genuine.

I related my thoughts to Ben, "I don't know why, but I believe Chuck knows these guys. When I mentioned this to Chuck, he shook his head, but something in his manner gives him away. I think he is lying, and he wasn't exactly thrilled to hear that they were caught. What do you think?"

"Yes, maybe so, but you can't jump to conclusions. You might be right. He hasn't talked about it much, but I don't think he had anything to do with it."

According to a newspaper report, Roswell Spencer was a chief investigator for the State's Attorney's Office and the man who arrested Frank Santucci. Mr. Santucci was arrested at the home of a former girlfriend that lived at 1701 N 35th Street. She was nursing Frank back to health. He had been wounded in the shoulder. The police claimed it was the bullet wound from the robbery.

Mr. Spencer also claimed that Miss Jean Hansen was once the girlfriend of Paul (Needlenose) Labriola, a hoodlum found poisoned and stuffed in a trunk of a car around 1954. Jean also had alliances with two other deceased hoodlums, James (Jingle Bells) Barsella and Martin (Marty the Ox) Ochs. Santucci was a known hoodlum associated with the Syndicate.

This information upset me. I showed Ben the paper. "Read this story, it's so far-fetched. Can these people be real?"

We were relieved to discover that the police had arrested the men. They would not be around to hold up other places. Several days later I was asked to come down to the police station to see if I could pick out Mr. Santucci in a lineup. I went willingly. I thought about the newspaper account and explained to the officer that I could not identify anyone because the men wore masks.

The officer seemed annoyed and said, "Yes, we know they wore masks. We also know who he is and I will point him out to you in the lineup.

"Don't you want to get these guys and put them away so they can't hurt anyone else?" he asked in frustration, "I can tell you, he is our man." He then showed me where Frank Santucci was in the lineup. "All you need to do is point to him. He is a bad guy and has hurt a lot of people. We need to take him off the street." He paused for a moment. "We can't do this without your testimony."

Frank claimed he had received his broken collarbone in a

gunfight the Saturday before. The authorities continued to maintain it was a gunshot wound he received in the holdup. I was glad to be of help. They explained that he was in a lineup with several plainclothes policemen and detectives. When they pointed Frank Santucci out to me; I pointed him out for the officers.

I said, "I hope he is the right person." They assured me he was. I was standing in front of the lineup with the police strongly pressuring me to identifying Frank Santucci. We could see each other. Both of us avoided eye contact. Because of my positive identification of Frank Santucci and Ret's positive identification of Robert Chesser, the three men were indicted for armed robbery and Ret and I would have to go to court.

I explained to Ben what had transpired at the police station.

He said, "I did not know they did things that way. I guess they are desperate to get this guy. You did the right thing."

I said, "I felt guilty when they spoke to me like that, as if I did not want them caught, but you know I do. The truth is I really could not identify him and what if it is the wrong guy?"

"Don't worry, Norma, these cops usually know what they are doing. I still think you did the right thing."

CHAPTER 8: CHUCK CRIMALDI

Chuck's attitude stuck in my mind. He appeared more than upset over the robbery and somehow I felt afraid, but did not understand why. My thoughts returned to when we first noticed him and remembered how we felt about him. We had decided to have a Friday night bartender as the owners before us had done. We used their choice of help for several months, but problems arose with this arrangement. Joe was a great guy, but he drank too much while working. We worried that trouble would break out and he would be in no condition to handle it. After Ben and Packy spoke to him, he took offense and quit.

We worked the place ourselves for several months and decided to find a replacement for Friday nights. Our place attracted other clientele besides factory workers. One fellow in particular caught our attention. Not exactly good looking, Chuck was about five-foot-seven, with blunt features and a slight build that did not conceal the fact that he was very strong. His black hair was receding; his dark brown eyes were sharp. Many times he stood alone looking around as if he was either planning to purchase the place or casing the premises. He was also in the building trade as a plumber and regularly came in for a drink after work. He was young and personable and got along with everyone.

Chuck frequented the bar every night and he seemed to have a following of people. He was very friendly and our husbands liked him, enjoying his company and sense of humor. They enjoyed a game of pool and he was a good competitor. He liked music and constantly played the jukebox, enjoying the same music as Ben. This created a friendship between the two. He had an infectious personality and mixed well with the old customers as well as the new.

I recalled that Joe had noticed our husbands being friendly with him and had emphasized that he was no good. He once stated, "You don't want to get tied up with the likes of him, he's bad news." We thought at the time that Joe was jealous and ignored his comment.

We discussed the possibility of hiring him for Friday nights. We laughed at ourselves, as our first impressions were superfluous. We were all in favor and when approached he was delighted and took the job.

The customers had a lot of comments and everyone wanted input into our business. When we hired Chuck Crimaldi, we received a lot of feedback, some of which was not positive. But it had been no different with Joe; it was difficult to please everyone.

Chuck drew a crowd, was witty, and had charisma. We assumed that because he was born and raised in a neighborhood not far from Albany Avenue that many of his followers were old friends. He had some respectable associates that held good jobs and dressed in suits and ties, but many of his friends were vulgar and uncouth. He kept them in line either with a glance or a word. We thought they either respected him or were afraid of him. He knew how to manipulate people with a smile. He did have strange acquaintances; but none of us could pinpoint what it was about him that bothered us.

"What do you think of Chuck?" I asked Ben after he had been working for us for several weeks. "Ret likes him, but Packy seems dubious. The other day these guys that work at the factory said they heard he had some connection to the Mafia. You know about the Mafia, don't you?"

Ben replied sarcastically, "Yes, I have heard of the Mafia. Chuck is a working guy just like us; that is just a rumor. You know every customer we have likes to think they are important and wants to be the favorite."

I responded, "I know, but growing up I heard of these organizations. Some people call them the Mafia, the Crime Syndicate or The Outfit, whatever name you wish to use. Most Italians are against these men and when you read the papers here, they talk about them all the time. The customers also said he works for a guy called Sam DeStefano. There are many stories about Sam in the newspaper. They say he is a man who loans money and charges high interest rates, more than banks. One customer said he uses torture to collect his loans and is not a nice man."

"Well, Norma, what do you think Chuck does in the Mafia? He is Italian, but he doesn't look the type to do much of anything. He is hardly 145 pounds. Look, he is a nice guy. I don't see it, and it doesn't interfere with our business. After all, every time he comes into the pub he is in dirty work clothes. He seems to be working all the time. If he works for this guy Sam, I don't know when. If you have noticed, he is always here or at his day job. Look, he is doing a good job and what he does in his own time is not our business."

"Yes, he does do a good job and is well-liked, but I do get concerned about who he associates with. We really don't want those kinds of people hanging around here. You know he has a girlfriend, I suppose he also needs to spend time with her." I replied.

"Lots of guys have a wife and a girlfriend. We don't have to like his lifestyle. Until we see something we don't like, you need to ignore the rumors. After all, he only works for four hours every Friday night. We do not treat him any different than anyone else who comes into the pub."

I replied, "Have you noticed how friendly he is with the policemen? He seems to know most of them. They hang around here sometimes. I heard that the police harass many of the other pubs, but not us. I wonder why?"

"Norma, he grew up in this area and probably knows them from that time. I don't know why and don't care. I am glad they don't bother us." Ben was becoming annoyed with me as my responses were challenging what he believed. I thought to myself that I probably did listen to too many rumors. I also was aware that the customers were really looking after our welfare. Most thought we were young and impressionable.

CHAPTER 9: PROPOSALS

Several weeks later, Chuck appeared worried as he approached us. He spoke with urgency. "I need to speak to you guys."

Ben was busy behind the bar, but responded, "Sure, but it is pretty hectic right now. Let me serve these guys first, then we can talk." Ben called me over and motioned for Packy to drop what he was doing and join us. After taking care of the customers, he turned his attention to Chuck. "What's up? It sounds important."

Chuck motioned for us to come into a corner of the pub near the kitchen. He picked a spot where we could converse and not be overheard.

That night the pub had many loud and noisy customers. His eyes darted quickly around the room twice, making sure no one could hear our conversation. He was anxious and tense, glancing in every direction, but did not look directly at us.

Ben said, "Make it quick, Chuck; we have a lot of people in here tonight." Ben rubbed his hands together indicating it was going to be a good night financially.

"I know, but this is important." We knew it had something to do with the robbery, otherwise what else could be this urgent.

He began his conversation, "I promised to put feelers out and I did. I spoke to Sam. He approached me because he knew I worked here. You know Sam who sometimes comes in here? Well, he is Sam DeStefano and knows a lot of people. Sam told me he wanted to help you out if he can. You know he likes to come in here for a drink and when he heard about the robbery, he was upset. He likes this place and likes you people. He wants all of you to come to his house to discuss the robbery. He really wants to help." Chuck's voice was tense and he was speaking rapidly to get his message across.

He continued, "Sam says he knows who did the robbery and told me he could get your money back." He paused and then said, "I know Sam. If he says he can help, he will." His words got our attention, this being the first indication that he knew Sam that well.

Sam DeStefano was a guy who stopped by the pub a few times. Ben told Packy and I, "This guy spends lots of money. For some reason Chuck is uptight when he is around." While reflecting on who Sam was, we remembered that Ben had indicated how edgy Chuck was around Sam. We thought it was because Sam was a wealthy guy and made people feel inferior that were less fortunate. Chuck gave us the impression that he preferred Sam would not come to our place. It appeared to make him uncomfortable.

Chuck continued, and spoke in a quiet voice. Shifting from one foot to the other he looked everywhere but not directly at us.

Ben questioned him, "If Sam was in this area, why didn't he come here and tell us himself? Why did he tell you?" Ben added, "Why doesn't he come here? You know how hard it is for all of us to get away at the same time. Besides, we need bartenders and babysitters. It is not that easy."

Ben was obviously agitated and raised his voice almost to a shout. He was not pleased that Chuck was the bearer of this news, knowing more about our circumstances than we did. Ben felt Sam should have spoken directly to us and not through a third party.

I looked at Ben and then Packy, it was apparent they were both frustrated with the whole situation. Chuck knew this was a big loss to us. He also knew Ben had a temper, so he began speaking softly in an effort to keep him calm.

"I know, I know, but I just happened to run into Sam. You know

Sam, he likes to do things in private and there are too many people around here." Chuck was still avoiding eye contact, but seemed sincere. He was extremely fidgety and on edge.

Ben replied in a quieter voice, "Thanks buddy, we will let you know. I need to take care of the bar right now." He tapped him on the shoulder in a friendly gesture and went behind the bar. Everyone was shouting for drinks. Packy and I jumped into help.

After the customers had left for the night, we talked amongst ourselves. Chuck had been exceptionally anxious and tense and we wondered why.

"This Sam guy really makes him uneasy. Chuck says that we know Sam, actually we don't know much about him at all. I think Chuck knows Sam better than we do. I have never seen him like that. I guess the only way we are going to find out is to see what Sam has to say. It would be interesting to see what he is all about."

Ben spoke quietly. Packy, Ben and I decided there was not any harm in hearing what he had to say. We asked ourselves the question, *Who was Sam?* All we knew was that Sam was this flashy guy who loved an audience and was supremely confident.

Packy said, "He likes to throw money around so everyone will think he is important. Most of these guys have never seen that much money and are in awe of him when he pulls that wad of bills out of his pocket."

Customers had told us that Sam often loaned money to people who were desperate or in a financial bind. When asked, Chuck spoke of Sam in a casual manner.

"Sam is really a good guy. He likes to help people and often comes into the neighborhood. Everyone knows Sam." He made it sound like Sam was a casual acquaintance.

"Do you recall when the guys from the factory told us we needed to be careful? Our place is hidden from the main street and a holdup is possible," Ben said to Packy and I.

We were naive and young and heeded this information too lightly. Our thoughts were that there were always too many people around and this could not happen.

CHAPTER 10: ARRANGING A MEETING

Sam came into the bar on several occasions; I saw him while serving other customers. He always sat near the front door in the corner with his back to the cigarette machine against the window. He was a man who stood about five-feet ten-inches with a slender build, weighing about 165 pounds. His sharp features and beady eyes caught our attention. He liked to dress in expensive attire to emphasize his importance and often wore dark glasses. I was told later that Sam wore glasses, although he did not need them, because he wanted people to think he had bad eyesight. He acted like he was straining his eyes as if he was trying to focus. He could see clearly and was actually sizing a person up. His voice was loud and he also liked to hold court, demanding everyone's attention. Sam drove a big, black Cadillac, a very expensive car. It was obvious he was not from this neighborhood.

Ben and Packy were always cordial to him. Sam was a big spender. It was apparent he was a shady character, possibly a small-time gangster. What we knew about him was only hearsay. He was a customer who only came around once in a while in the evening. Ret did not know him. Everyone who spoke to him addressed him as Mister DeStefano. At this point I had not formed an opinion about him, but knew I did not like his manner.

Ret and I discussed our options as to what our decision should be. "Let the boys make the decision," I said. "I am not sure I want to meet him at his place, but Ben thinks we should see what he has to say." Ret smiled, "Packy feels the same. He said, 'What have we got to lose?'"

CHAPTER 11: DATE WITH THE DEVIL

Chuck smiled broadly and looked relieved when we informed him of our decision. The worried expression he had seemed to disappear.

Grinning, he said, "Great, I'll let Sam know and make the arrangements." He was upbeat, strutting around the bar making conversation, and cracking jokes with everyone. It seemed a weight had been lifted off his shoulders.

Ret and I made arrangements for the care of our children. The boys had a friend who would take over the bar.

Ben said, "We will only be gone for a couple of hours." It was at this point that we began to realize that Chuck had more of a connection with Sam than we had thought. When he came to escort us to Sam's home, he appeared uneasy.

They arranged the time and date of the meeting. Sam DeStefano and his family lived in an upscale neighborhood near Harlem and North Avenue at 1656 N Sayre Street. We still questioned why Chuck took such an interest and wondered what his connection to the robbery was. Somehow his explanation did not seem authentic. Chuck led the way and we followed in our car. He knew the route well, as if he had taken it many times.

We talked about Sam. I said, "I have only seen Sam a few times. There is something about him I do not like. He is always loud. He doesn't stare at you. He stares through you."

Ret laughed.

Ben said, "Don't be so silly."

"I am not being silly; I just don't like him. He thinks spending money around the bar impresses everyone. He is arrogant."

Ben chuckled, "You are being silly."

Packy piped in, "Who cares, let him spend his money."

There was a parking space in front of Sam's house. We were somewhat disappointed that it was an ordinary house and not very fancy. I think we were expecting a luxurious mansion. The house was stucco and a drab grey color. It had small windowpanes and was old-fashioned. We climbed the few steps to the front door where Sam's wife Anita greeted us. She was a small, attractive woman with dark hair and a pleasant face.

Holding out her hand, she said, "I am Sam's wife, please come in." We smiled at her. She seemed so nice.

Though we had never met her, Chuck seemed to know her very well. They appeared to be good friends. She smiled back at us as she greeted him, hugged him firmly with affection and kissed his cheek. Anita led us into the living room where Sam was sitting in an overstuffed armchair. He was not dressed, but was wearing a bathrobe and slippers, which caught us off guard. He did not greet us or rise, but told us in a gruff voice to sit down. It soon became apparent that this was not a social visit.

The chairs were arranged in a row facing him; each of us took a seat. Sam sat across the room staring at us. The living room was quite dark. Dim lights were placed around the room, casting shadows on the walls.

Chuck was pacing anxiously behind us and Anita was fluttering around trying to look inconspicuous. Looking up at the shadows on the wall, the images looked like puppets dancing in a nervous fashion.

There were not too many pleasantries and Sam began speaking, painting a portrait of himself as a real nice guy. He had one of those gravelly voices that reminded me of sandpaper. His story began by telling us how tough he had it growing up. His first job was working in apartment buildings cleaning toilets and doing menial jobs.

"I was a janitor," he snarled, "Now I own the apartments." Gloating, he explained how it had taken him years to accomplish his goals. He boasted, "I am a businessman. I had to fight and crawl to get to my position. I know what hard work is." He pounded his chest. Once he believed he had established himself in our eyes, he turned his attention to us.

He acknowledged that he heard we had a little problem. He exclaimed, "I want to help you get your money back and help the men accused of robbing your place at the same time."

He emphasized, "There is nothing in this for me personally. I like to help people and I feel I can be of assistance making the problem disappear."

Sam smiled, "No one needs problems. I know the men personally who were indicted for the robbery and I can tell you they made a mistake. They are nice guys and it would be a shame if they were convicted. They have families and would probably get ten years in the penitentiary." He threw his arms in the air. "Ten years. Do you know how long ten years is in a prison?" he repeated, but did not wait for a response.

He rambled on, "They came to me and asked if I could help them. I have known them since they were boys." This was a questionable statement; Donato was over fifty years old. Sam wasn't much older.

"These men have trouble finding decent jobs to support their families. They have no *education*, " he stressed. He paused to observe us, making sure he had captivated our interest. "I told them I knew you people. You were nice folks and I was sure you would be reasonable."

He went on, "I explained to them that you were young couples with families who have a small business. You need your money to run the business. You folks are just starting out. Business is tough; everyone needs their few dollars. They should not have been there at your place, but sometimes people get desperate. They are desperate men and did not want to hurt anyone. They are sorry."

Sam paused; cleared his throat and spit into an ashtray nearby, staring at us with intensity. His eyes were narrow slits. He studied us for a few more moments. His face was blank, probably wondering if he was getting through to us. At first he spoke quietly, we could hardly hear him. Suddenly he raised his voice in a loud, harsh manner. We all jumped to attention and I nearly fell out of my chair.

"Ten years is a long time to be away from your family for a little mistake. They are prepared to give you the money back if you will drop the charges."

None of us had spoken; he had our attention. He continued staring at us, and then smiled.

"All you have to do is not give a positive identification. You could say, 'I am not sure. He looks like the guy. He could be the guy, but I'm not sure.' After all, ten years is a stiff sentence and they are not bad boys, only foolish." He paused, studied our faces, "I am afraid that something bad could happen to any one of you and I cannot protect you"

I thought, *protect us from what*? If we helped put the robbers in jail, why would we need protection?

His voice became gruff and potent, shouting in a loud, booming voice. Whether he was aware or not, his robe fell partially open, revealing that he did not have much on underneath.

Watching him carefully, I felt concern for Ret because she was the one that could identify the one man. As he spoke, his manner became more forceful and bold. Obviously he was used to getting his own way. I believed our silence annoyed him. He had to convince us that he was being helpful in our interest.

47

Suddenly, he leapt from his chair and began muttering with deep, guttural sounds. His body hunched over and he began speaking to the ground as if he were communicating with Satan. His face was contorted, twisted in a strange manner, and it was frightening. He became uglier and uglier and my mind began to race as I stared at him, until I no longer could hear his words. It was as if he were speaking in a foreign tongue.

I felt a chill run down my spine; he was repulsive. As he spoke, he looked like a man possessed. Everyone was tense. We all sat up straight and it seemed as if the room stood still. Glancing at one another, we did not say a word. I reached for Ben's hand. The men's expressions were blank and all of us stared with intensity. I sensed that my eyes were bulging out of my head.

We had heard many things about Sam. Some people said he was ruthless, others said he was crazy. Whatever he was, I just knew we had to get out of there. There was something dark and menacing about that house. Sam's movements and the way he spoke, waving his arms around like a madman, gave him a sinister aura.

As he continued his everlasting monologue, his expressions became more depraved. His mouth twisted to the side as he drooled. He wiped the drool away with his sleeve, his eyes bulging out of their sockets as he stared at us.

The whole time that Chuck paced behind us, I wondered what he was thinking and wished I could see his expressions. Was he aware that Sam was like this? He had never given us any indication. Sam's language became revolting and inappropriate, cursing and swearing like a drunken sailor.

He continued talking to the devil, using profanities, and sitting down then rising again from his chair. He began pacing the floor and the incoherent rambling continued.

"You do not have to identify the man, only say it looked like the man. I am not sure if it is the man. It could be the man. I am not sure. Everyone makes mistakes," he made gestures like a play actor in a part; "It is hard making a living for a family, these boys just made a mistake," he shouted in a croaky voice.

Suddenly he was quiet. When he spoke, his voice was hoarse, and the words were illogical. Chuck was still pacing and Anita was anxious, unsure of what he would do next. The room was silent. Sam slumped over in his chair and looked exhausted. For some reason, the lights in the room suddenly seemed brighter. Chuck and Anita were talking behind us, but I could not decipher what was said. This whole meeting was surreal.

The stillness lasted for several minutes. Ben rose quickly from his seat and spoke, breaking our silence. We had been sitting there for nearly two hours.

He was polite, "Thanks for wanting to help us, but we need to go now and take care of our business. Of course, we need to discuss this amongst ourselves and will let you know."

He added, "We will let Chuck know what we decide." He motioned for us to rise as he spoke with confidence and authority. Packy motioned in agreement. We followed him to the door like lambs.

I nearly tripped over my own feet, trying to reach the door in a hurry. Packy was quiet. Ret had a look of awe as if she had imagined the whole thing. This was not the answer Sam wanted. As we walked out the door, he was still trying to convince us of the decision we should make.

"After all," he shouted in his gravelly voice, "I cannot give you any guarantee as to what could happen to you. Ten years is a long time. These guys are sorry and hoped you would help them."

Sometime later we learned that Sam was not pleased with the robbery. The men who had robbed our place picked a place where his employee Chuck worked. It was suggested that this would bring heat on the outfit and Sam. We were unaware that the police and the State's Attorney's Office were aware that Chuck was associated with Sam.

We said goodnight and Chuck left at the same time as we did. He twisted his body around and embraced Anita who was standing at the door, saying, "See you soon."

He turned to us and said in flippantly, "Sam gets carried away sometimes. Don't take him too serious. He likes to be dramatic. He likes you guys. Look, I'll see you later; I have some things I have to take care of." He was uneasy, but trying very hard to be cool and lighthearted.

We drove back to the tavern. Ret said quietly, "I know what you mean," referring to Sam. The rest of the ride home was in silence; we all had a lot to think about. It had been an uncomfortable situation and all of us wondered how Chuck fit into all of this.

I checked on the kids and helped Ben in the bar until it closed. I felt the need to talk and did not want to be by myself. After the last customer was gone, we retired to our apartment. I prepared a cup of tea and fixed a snack. We sat together in silence, both of us preoccupied with our own thoughts. As we reflected on the evening, it seemed like a movie, a horror movie.

Ben was the first to speak, "That guy is nuts. I actually was a little scared in that house."

"I was scared, too. I can't understand why Chuck is so friendly with him. Do you think it's because he is scared? Sam worships the devil. His language was appalling; it sent shivers down my spine." I looked at Ben. "The only thing he lacked was horns." I was trying to be funny by inserting a little humor, but Ben looked serious.

"I think we are over our heads and I am worried where this is going to lead."

I agreed. "I thought his wife was so nice. I couldn't believe what we were hearing. Chuck and Anita were so nervous. That house felt evil." I paused for a second, "You know, I still think Chuck knows more than he lets on. He is not honest with us. Me, I don't trust him."

Ben was deep in thought. He said, "I don't know." He added, "Chuck has never spoken very much about Sam. It seems he does know more than he lets on. I don't know what to think. I have never seen anyone act like that. The guy is crazy." He paused, "We need to take this serious. Whatever you and Ret decide to do, you know I will stand by your decision."

I said, "Ben, I know this is serious and it frightens me, but it's up to Ret. Whatever she decides, we will stand by her. I would hate to be in her shoes. I know she is scared."

CHAPTER 12: OUR DECISION

Ret and I debated back and forth as to what to do. The burden was on Ret and my heart went out to her. She could identify Robert Chesser, the man who sat at the bar that day. I knew I could recant my statement about Santucci because they wore masks.

I said to her, "You know this is up to you, I can't identify anyone."

She said, "I know."

Chuck seemed anxious and worried that we would not accept Sam's offer. We would look at him and wonder who he was.

Most of the time he seemed like a nice person, sometimes he was a bit quirky. Some of the people he associated with were unsavory. Personally, we did not know very much about him. But in the pub business, these things were matter of fact. There were many strange things about him. We still could not put our finger on what it was and that was troubling.

Chuck was tense and edgy a lot of the time and had quiet conversations on the phone. He would whisper as if he did not want anyone to hear. He was very secretive, receiving frequent phone calls while in the bar, whether he was working or not. This habit was beginning to irk me. I felt he needed to curtail his calls. They did not pertain to our business. It was annoying and was getting on my nerves. I related my feeling to Ben.

He said, "You have been through a lot and you need to get a hold of yourself. You are just upset. You are blaming everyone for what has happened. Chuck is only trying to help."

"I have been through a lot, but I am a realist. You know, Ben, I am tired of you always protecting these people. Why do you feel that you owe Chuck this sense of loyalty? Chuck is not as honest with you as you think, so don't preach to me. He is getting on my nerves and so are you."

It appeared that what we would decide did not matter. Sam had made the choice for us. The visit at his home was unsettling. We were nervous and worried. Ret and I discussed the situation for several days and wondered what we should do. I thought about the lineup, it was not like the ones that are portrayed on television. There was no glass to protect your identity. I sat in front of the lineup several feet away as the officers explained to me who was in the lineup. The men assembled in the lineup could see me and vice versa. Once when looking back, Frank Santucci was staring at me as if he hated me. I didn't even know him.

The next day the telephone calls began, whispered messages such as "I am going to kill you." "We know where your children go to school." Sometimes the caller used profanity in a deep, husky voice graphically describing all the things that could happen. Other times there was just deep breathing on the phone. These calls came several times a day and it was unnerving. They continued for several days and I was afraid to answer the phone. They were coming to the bar phone and the house phone, it was scary.

The last straw was when our youngest daughter Patricia answered the phone. She was frightened and said, "Mommy, someone said they are going to kill me."

I was angry and reassured her it was a prank call and said to her, "Sometimes people are not nice."

I confronted Chuck. "What the hell is going on with these phone calls?" He looked at me with a blank stare as if he did not know what I was talking about.

"What phone calls?" He insisted that he did not understand and said "Sam would not make calls like that. He's not that kind of a guy."

"Really," I replied. "Someone is not happy about this whole thing."

Chuck replied, "It's probably the guys that robbed the place, who else would it be? You know they are scared."

I did not respond.

Why was he protecting Sam? Nothing made any sense. Somehow I did not believe him; the look in his eyes betrayed him.

The strange conversation at Sam's house disturbed me. He talked to the devil. He was evil. Surely Chuck knew more about Sam than he let on. He knew where he lived; he must have been at that house before. He was friendly with Sam's wife. What was Chuck's secret? We were frightened; it would be an understatement to say we were not. Our children were innocent. We were worried and afraid for them as well as for ourselves.

After many days of discussion, Ret said, "Packy and I have thought it over and decided I'll not make a positive identification."

"Are you sure this is what you want to do?" I asked, feeling anxious.

She replied, "Yes, it's what I have to do."

Packy said in defiance, "Sam is nuts and I wish Ret had never identified that guy, but she did. We decided to do what's best for all of us. I am not afraid to go up to Sam's house and get the money. It's our money."

I said. "Well, I will never go to that house again. To tell the truth, I was afraid."

Packy laughed at me and was kidding when he said, "Come on, you are not scared of anything."

Together our decision was to take the bribe. It was unanimous. Ret would not give a positive identification and our lives would continue. It was not a good option, but all of us were relieved that a conclusion had been reached. I once was told everyone had a price and I guess we were no exception.

Chuck was elated when we told him and suddenly the phone calls stopped. His whole demeanor changed, plus he became like the old Chuck, cheerfully interacting with the customers or indulging in a game of pool and cracking a few jokes. Chuck was a happier man. It did not go unobserved by us and we were puzzled. Packy picked up $1100 from Sam's home and returned the money to the cash box.

He said, "Here is the money, Norma, I will just put it in the box."

I smiled at him. "Thanks."

We never discussed it again.

CHAPTER 13: END OF A PARTNERSHIP

It was sometime after New Year's in 1963 and several weeks after our visit with Sam that our partners said they wanted to speak to us. Their behavior for the last few months had been uptight and strained.

"What is it you want to talk about?" Ben asked.

Packy cleared his throat and blurted out, "We decided we would like to pack in the bar business. It is not what I thought it was going to be. We just want out." He continued, "Ret and I have discussed this for some time, even before the Sam thing. We decided this is what we would like to do."

Then Ret said, "The pub is not for us. Packy's not cut out for the business and I want to have a social life."

We were caught off guard and certainly did not expect this announcement. At the same time, however, we were not surprised. There were many incidents that had cropped up and were not resolved.

The customers told us that that Packy had closed the bar early many nights when we were on vacation. He was also unhappy that Ret had to stay at the pub into the afternoons. He was a jealous man and did not like her interacting with the customers as much as she did. This put a strain on their relationship. His actions put a strain on all of us.

The holdup was the turning point in our lives and in our relationship. We became very aware of what could happen in this business, but we had an investment. If we could not sell the tavern, one of us had to take over.

Packy said, "I have put these figures together. This is what you owe us and we can call it quits." They offered us a deal that was not favorable to us. In fact, we thought it was unreasonable.

I studied the paper for several minutes and then Packy said, "Well, look it over and we can talk about it tomorrow." Later that evening I explained to Ben what their proposal was.

I said, "We will give them half of the money on hand and the cost of stock that has been paid. We can also give some money for the value of the partnership. That would be fair."

Ben agreed and explained to Packy, "These are our terms; otherwise we will give you the pub and take the same terms you offered us." We stood firm on our decision.

Their final decision was that they truly wanted out and accepted our terms. None of us were happy. It was a stressful situation because more funds did not exist. We had entered this partnership with very little money. Ben and I accepted the responsibility of the pub. I would have liked to throw in the towel, as they were prepared to do, but everything we owned was tied up in the tavern. It was not going to be easy.

After the details were settled, they purchased a house in the suburbs. We did not see much of them after that, but we kept in touch since there was still a court date to face. In reality, there was not enough income for two large families. We changed the name of the pub from B and P. Tap to Ben's Place.

CHAPTER 14: BEN'S PLACE & ART

After our partners departed, Ben and I worked together for a while. I took care of the kitchen and he looked after the bar. We hired Stacy, a lady who lived a few doors away, to help serve the lunches. She was a large woman with many children. She had a nice personality and needed the money. It was a good arrangement.

Art Stark was a truck driver who frequented the bar on a daily basis. Initially, Art was just a customer. Soon we became friends and eventually he began to assist me in the bar. Because he had owned his own bar, he was very helpful. Even though Art was in his fifties, he had jet-black hair. He stood about five-feet five-inches tall, had a stocky build and very strong. I liked to tease him about his protruding stomach. He would laugh at me.

"You should have seen me when I was your age. I was a heart breaker. What do you think about that?"

Laughing, I would respond, "I think you are kidding me."

With Ret and Packy gone, Ben eventually returned to work as a bricklayer. He decided that he did not want to be around the bar all day. Customers were offended if he did not accept a drink from them.

"If you and Art can handle everything, I want to go back to work. The bar is to confining and I need the diversion."

I ran the bar and Art helped out in peak times. He was a supervisor for his company. He did most of his own work as a truck driver in the morning. At lunchtime he came to the pub to help out and then left to finish his runs. There was a lot of cleaning to do after lunch and kids to take care of. Art returned in the afternoon so I could pick up the children from school. His buddy Albert, another truck driver, was usually with him. Albert was Stacy's brother. He came to visit his sister every day and often assisted us.

Art noticed how overwhelmed I was with the busy bar and noted I could not keep up with the action.

He loved to tease me, "Come on, I will help you. I told Ben I would give you a hand. Do you think you have ten arms and can do everything by yourself?" I hated to ask for his assistance because he refused to accept any pay. But he loved getting a sandwich and a couple pints of beer.

I said, "No one works for nothing. I don't mind paying you something, anything." He would ignore me and carry on with whatever he was doing.

He once said, "You are like one of my kids." Art was like a father to me and if I had errands to run, he was there. He also stayed until Ben returned in the evening to make sure the children and I were safe.

Art was the father of eight children. While he was stationed overseas during the Second World War, his wife passed away and his children were put in an orphanage. When he returned, he tried unsuccessfully to get his children back. The state government told him that he had to provide a stable home before the children would be released to him. He married a second time and took charge of his children. However, his second marriage failed. He had bought a pub and his new wife liked the pub better than a family. Art would marry again and have a daughter. He passed away in the year 2002 at the age of 88.

Younger couples were moving into the area, having recently migrated from the South. Our clientele in the evenings brought in nearly as many women as men as new faces appeared. They were happy people and the pub took on a different atmosphere.

Ben kept the fun going. He sang songs from behind the bar while he served the customers. Mack the Knife became his theme song and he had all of Bobby Darin's actions down solid. The ladies who came to the pub would swoon and I am not sure if I wasn't perhaps a little jealous. I was envious that Ben had such an easy way with people. He encouraged customers to dance and soon we had a younger mixed crowd coming to our place. The pub became his entertainment.

We were entirely different in our personalities. Ben would say, "You are the straight guy and I am the funny guy." We had a lot in common, but we were as different as night and day. Ben worried me. He did not see the serious side of things, trusting too many people as if they were family. I, on the other hand, was more dubious. He would say "It's all for the business, Norma. Look at all the new customers we have, this is the fun place." It *was* a fun place; there was no arguing that point.

Ben enjoyed the role of playing matchmaker among our pub patrons. We had many single men and women who came to the pub. They were looking for a good time and a partner would be nice. For instance, Sam Pittman was a bricklayer who worked with Ben on many jobs and Judy was a divorced mother with three young girls.

Both were tall, good-looking people. When Ben introduced them, they liked each other immediately. Soon they became inseparable and eventually we had a wedding. Unfortunately, the marriage did not last. Judy wanted a husband and father, and Sam did not know how to appreciate a family. The pub was still his home.

Chuck Johnson was a young, handsome chap from the South. He had a good job as a tool and die maker. He was short and stood only five-feet four-inches tall. He must have had his heart broken at one time as he always played sorrowful songs on the jukebox. He would also drink himself into oblivion, laying his head on the bar to sleep. Ben introduced him to Geneva, a lovely, buxom brunette. At five-feet ten-inches, Geneva was a lonely girl and was much taller than Chuck. They made an awkward couple on the dance floor; his head only came up to her bosom. He would lay his head on her chest and it appeared she was holding him up.

Ben also introduced Charles and Laura. Laura was a waitress at the Ohio Inn, a tavern across the street from Albany Avenue. She had an unhappy romance where her boyfriend conned her out of a large sum of money. When he eventually disappeared, Laura was devastated. She was lonely and enjoyed our pub better than her place of employment. We were the fun place. After she spent countless evenings playing love songs on the jukebox, Ben introduced Laura to Charles. He was a quiet guy who had a good job. Ben managed to help form romances with these couples. He would kid them on and sing romantic songs. They loved it.

Soon these couples got married. They would return to the tavern after their ceremony and we would have a party. The pub would be decorated with balloons and confetti. We would put up a nice spread for the happy couple. Many of the bar patrons helped celebrate the event. We became their home away from home. I would just shake my head. Art said to me, "You have to give Ben credit; he knows how to get people together. These weddings are good for business."

We took pride in our business, always having something going on such as a birthday party, an anniversary, or any excuse for a party. I enjoyed a dance or two, but I was more reserved. We had competitions on the pool table to keep the fun going with cash prizes. I also learned to play pool and became very competitive. It was all in the spirit of good relations with the customers. We would also roll the dice for the jukebox. Each person would put in a quarter and the highest number on the dice would win. They would keep half of the money for themselves and half for the jukebox. The jukebox never stopped playing. We all learned to dance the twist. This was our best year and a fun year, but things would change.

CHAPTER 15: COURT

One year later, in July of 1963, we went to court. Ret and I met at the pub and drove together. We did not speak much on our way there, both of us lost in our own thoughts. We were anxious as we arrived at the courthouse. I felt tense as the prosecutor gave us final instructions of what we were supposed to say. I wondered if Ret was having second thoughts. I glanced at her. Her head was bent low, as if she was praying. She looked up when the prosecutor addressed her.

He said, "Are you okay? Don't be nervous. These guys can't hurt you."

I thought to myself, "That's what you think." She shook her head.

I was the first to go on the witness stand and felt terrified. There was this uneasy, panicky feeling in my chest. Clearing my throat and praying my voice would not crack, I raised my right hand.

The question was asked, "Can you see the men who robbed your premises in this courtroom?"

I responded quietly, "The men wore masks, I cannot identify them." My voice was hoarse and my knees shook.

The attorney shouted, "Speak up."

Taking a drink of water, I cleared my throat, sat up right and looked straight ahead not wanting to see the three suspects. I repeated, "The men wore masks, I could not see their faces." I could feel the prosecutor's eyes on me. I sat quietly, looking down at my feet.

He paused for several minutes then said. "I have no more questions." The defense did not have any questions, either. I was dismissed.

Ret was next on the stand. I looked at her, hoping to give her moral support, but she stared straight ahead. She was sworn in. I sat in anticipation and wondered what her testimony would be. Many times on the phone we had discussed what we would or would not say. We could no longer joke around about our options; this was real and serious.

When the prosecutor handed Ret the photo of Mr. Robert Chesser, she looked at it as if she were seeing it for the first time.

Her voice quivering, she said, "I am not sure if this picture is of the man I saw. It looks like him, but I cannot say for sure if it is the man." Her Scottish accent seemed more pronounced.

The prosecutor questioned, "Did you not identify this man in this picture before?"

Ret replied, her head bent low. "I thought it was the man, but now I am not sure." It was painful for her to lie under oath.

The prosecuting attorney was irritated and annoyed. He said loudly, "Look at the photo again." Ret shook her head. There were tears in her eyes. She was dismissed.

The prosecutor was frustrated and angry. He did not say anything, but threw his papers down on the desk. He stared at us; the case was over. We scurried from the courtroom with our heads bent low, wishing we were invisible. We had wasted their time. They knew someone had gotten to us. They were so sure they had a conviction. They were disappointed and we felt sick at what we had done. But protecting our families was our priority. The judge acquitted the men. Nobody was happy about the outcome, except the three men and Sam.

We fled from the courtroom. Ret and I ran down the courtroom stairs, holding hands so as not to trip. Neither one of us had anything to say. We looked over and saw the three crooks laughing and jeering at us. We were heartsick; they were guilty and we let them get away. It was over. Our fears were not over, but the incident was. We would put the whole thing behind us. It would be fair to say that as long as Chuck was around, we never had another holdup.

CHAPTER 16: YEAR OF UNREST

In 1963, we had our best year financially. We worked seven days a week and the hours were endless. The returns on the business were exceptional. I said, "Look, we have made over $35,000 this year, isn't that great?"

Ben smiled, "Well, we have worked hard for it." Once again we had a personal bank account.

However, the country was not doing so great. First the court case, then there was the assassination of President Kennedy on November 22, 1963. It was a sad day.

Everyone in the pub had their eyes glued to the television set. The atmosphere in the tavern was gloomy. People who were not interested in politics suddenly could not get enough of the story. Everyone was depressed and could not understand how this could happen in their country. The fun and games had stopped. It did not matter what religion, race or ethnicity you were. Everyone was upset and had an opinion.

The bar buzzed with speculation about who was responsible for the assassination. Of course, the Mafia was named as one of the perpetrators. The name Jack Ruby was also on everyone's lips since he came from Chicago. I was upset at being of Italian descent because it seemed Italians were always connected to the Mafia. Mostly they were portrayed as violent gangsters and this troubled me. I related this to my mother once, who said, "There are Italians and there are Italians. There are good and bad people in every race."

She kept everything simple.

I thought about the Italian people I was raised with. Most of them lived in a section of the Trail in an area called The Gulch on Rossland Avenue. The Gulch was Little Italy. We lived in this area until I was five. As one drove down the avenue, the railway tracks were situated to the left and the Catholic church stood proud and tall surrounded by small houses. To the right were high cliffs with houses built into crevices in the rock. The roads to these houses were steep and narrow. When I later passed the house where we had lived, the one with the veranda, I remember wondering how it would have been if we had stayed a part of this community.

I recalled how the shops were owned or managed by Italians. The language was complex for them, so they banded together and found friendship and support in each other. They shared interests such as food, music, religion and sense of humor. Everybody congregated on the street. People exchanged news from home, argued politics and their conversations continued for hours. Shopkeepers did well selling their wares and many were imported goods from Italy. The people were delighted with their selection. Young men with accordions played music in the street and children danced. The bars in the area did a roaring business. It was not unusual to see a man sitting on the sidewalk, unable to function because he had consumed too much alcohol. Someone who knew him would take him home. The people in The Gulch took care of one another. These were the Italians I knew.

1963 was also the year of the race riots. Because we were situated quite close to Madison Street where the majority of the activity was taking place, we knew we had to take some precautions. This uprising and unrest was in the areas of Madison Street and Humboldt Park. African-Americans and Puerto Ricans went on a spree of looting and arson in the commercial areas.

With the chaos in the area, security procedures were taken. Our first priority was to make certain the buzzer on the entrance worked properly. We used it to allow only patrons we knew to enter the bar. The safety of our children was our biggest concern.

Their school was located in an African-American neighborhood, so we made it a priority to escort them to and from school. Race had never been an issue in our pub and interracial friendships flourished in our neighborhood. Despite this, we knew that race was a big problem in the United States and this made us uneasy.

During these times, Ben worked just in the bar to ensure our safety. "Its better I am here," he said, "until this blows over."

One of our customers had a sporting business on Madison Street. During the riots, rocks were thrown and shattered the front window and the merchandise in the store was looted. The contents were removed in shopping carts by the rioters and the police could not stop them. The store was then set ablaze. Everything was lost.

CHAPTER 17: CAROLE & CHUCK

As time proceeded, the dark side of Chuck's personality asserted itself. This showed in the despicable way he treated his girlfriend, Carole. Once again, Chuck continued to whisper to his friends and when either one of us entered the premises or were in hearing distance, the conversation stopped. He would walk away, cracking a joke as if nothing was going on. It disturbed us more each day.

"Have you noticed every time we come into the room, Chuck changes the subject. I can't imagine what all the whispering is about. I think he is getting too comfortable here."

Ben agreed, "Recently he hasn't taken me into his confidence, but he has been acting a little erratic. The other night when he came into work with Carole, she sat at the end of the bar. I thought that that was peculiar as she usually sits in the middle of the bar. I noticed him looking around. He was acting strange, but he does that sometimes. When he thought no one was looking, he took a gun out of his pocket and gave it to her. She slipped the gun into her handbag. I was startled, but didn't say anything. He was being sneaky. I stayed downstairs that night to see if anything was going on. Do you remember when I said it was busy and I would stay downstairs to help in the bar?"

I was alarmed. "I wonder why he is carrying a gun?"

Ben shrugged his shoulders.

"I don't know, but nothing happened. You know several of the guys that come in the pub carry guns."

Carole seemed like a nice person. She was slim, attractive, and well groomed and her dresses were impeccable. Her auburn hair was stylish. She was slightly taller than Chuck. A quiet girl, she kept to herself. Throughout the night, Carole would dig in her purse and pull out a handful of pills. She claimed they were for her allergies. Her glazed eyes often looked vacant. When she laughed, which was not often, it sounded empty. Each time she put her hand into her pocketbook, I thought about the gun.

Chuck watched her every movement and glared at everyone who spoke to or looked at her. He never said a word, but his eyes gave away his uncertainties. He was possessive and found reasons to start a confrontation with anyone who paid too much attention to her. Most men backed away.

She never spoke much and usually sat quietly in the bar. Her eyes followed his every move. Whether he was playing pool or was on the other side of the bar as the bartender, Carole watched him. She would nurse a couple of drinks for the entire evening, only speaking when someone spoke to her. Her words were chosen carefully and her conversations lacked substance. Everyone knew she was Chuck's girl.

We knew Chuck had married young and had heard he had marital problems. Someone said he had four children. He was twenty-eight, the same age as me. We did not ask about his personal life, nor did he volunteer the information. Carole came to the bar with him on all occasions as if she were his wife.

One night at closing time, the bar was empty. Most customers had gone home or were on their way to the four o'clock joint, Pat and Joe's. Chuck and Carole were the last people to leave. They were sitting in a corner of the bar, their heads bent, having a heated argument. Bobby Lochheed, a friend of Ben's who also came from Scotland, sat at the other end of the bar. They were enjoying a drink and having a conversation. Chuck and Carole's argument soon became loud and crude. Suddenly, Chuck jumped up in anger and overturned several stools. Both men looked up in time to witness Chuck standing over Carole punching her face.

She was crouched into a corner covering her face, trying to soften the blows, but he was vicious. He started tearing into her as if she were a punching bag. Carole was hysterical. Ben hurried to the other end of the bar, trying to talk to him. He pulled Chuck off Carole, who was sobbing loudly trying to catch her breath. Chuck was enraged.

"What the hell are you doing? Come on Chuck, she is a girl, take it easy." Ben's efforts were ignored. Bobby jumped up and went to Carole's defense.

Bobby punched Chuck. Like a man possessed, Chuck reacted swiftly with deadly intentions. He scooped up a cue ball from the pool table and started swinging at Bobby with the ball wrapped in his fist. Chuck was unable to clearly strike Bobby, but scuffled for a few minutes. Ben successfully separated them. Chuck looked at Bobby with eyes full of hate. He darted out of the bar to his car and moments later returned with a baseball bat.

At closing, if Ben had not come upstairs, I would go down to pick up the money from the till. Hearing the noise and commotion as stools were being overturned; I knew there was trouble. My thoughts began to run wild with the fear that someone may have been hurt. I stopped short behind the half door by the kitchen where only my head would be visible. I saw Chuck with the baseball bat standing in front of Bobby ready to strike him. Ben interceded and began wrestling with Chuck to prevent him from swinging the bat. I could see Carole crouched in the corner sobbing. Chuck's face was contorted, displaying nothing but hate.

Ben looked up when he realized I was there and shouted, "Go back upstairs," Chuck stopped and looked in the direction of the door, suddenly lowering the bat.

Chuck cooled down quickly and began helping Ben pick up the

stools then sat down. He appeared embarrassed and apologized for his outburst, fluffing it off with a hand gesture.

"I am sorry I lost my temper. You know how women are. She really got me riled up," he explained. "Look, I'll see you at Pat and Joe's." Turning to Carole, he smiled, "Come darling, Ben needs to close." Carole looked frightened as she picked up her purse. She was still visibly shaken, but gathered her things and they left the bar together. Chuck put his arm around her to show his affection.

Bobby was pretty shaken up, "God, Ben," he said, "That guy is nuts. You need to be careful."

"I know," Ben said joking, "but you know the old expression, you can't interfere with a man and his woman. They turn on you even if your intentions are good." He added, "Seriously, I will be careful, he's a guy you don't want to mess with." Bobby left a short time later and went home.

Ben closed the bar. He went to Pat and Joe's where he met up with Chuck and Carole. Chuck shouted for him to come and sit with them in the booth. Ben motioned for the bartender and bought them a drink. They sat for a while in silence. Ben acknowledged other people he knew. Then he brought up the incident that had occurred earlier.

"You know, my friend was just defending a woman as that is his style. It was not his intention to interfere."

Chuck was defensive. "I don't need anyone involving themselves in my personal business. He doesn't know me and he should mind his own business."

Ben replied, "No one interferes in your personal life and that's all very well, but I am not going to have someone injured in my bar because you can't control your temper. I hope it won't happen again."

Chuck looked down then nodded his head and did not reply. They drank their drinks in silence. Ben excused himself and left,

"See you later," he said to Chuck,

"Ben, look I am sorry," he muttered. The subject was dropped. Ben's friend did not know how lucky he had been. Chuck's style was not to forget any incident.

The next morning, Ben said, "Chuck stopped because he thought you were Donna." Bobby received a reprieve that night.

CHAPTER 18: SUSPICIOUS

After that episode, Ben became more wary of Chuck. He acted as if it had never happened. Ben remembered another time when there had been an argument on the pool table. There was a scuffle and Chuck came from behind the bar to break it up. With one punch, he knocked the man out. The customers were very impressed. Ben found out later that Chuck had a pool ball in his hand. It was not just a lucky punch.

Looking back, he also recalled the episode with Chuck's friend, Frank Arnuri. It was in September of 1961, shortly after the birth of our son Martin. I had injured my back quite severely lifting the liquor boxes that had just been delivered. It annoyed me because the boxes were still sitting on the floor blocking the doorway. With Ben no longer available during the day to do the heavy lifting and since Ret had gone home early, I foolishly attempted to move them myself. I spent many weeks in the hospital in traction as a result.

Our husbands had good bricklayer jobs that they wanted to hold on to. They agreed to hire Chuck's friend to assist in the bar until things returned to normal. Ben spoke to Chuck about Frank, "Do you think he is capable of bartending until Norma gets home?" Jokingly, he inquired, "Can he count?"

Chuck replied seriously, "I will vouch for him. He is a stand up guy, he's good and I will see that he does a good job. Did you know he used to own his own bar?" Chuck seemed sincere. Frank and Chuck's father-in-law, Tory, were friends, but neither seemed to have a job.

I did not approve of Frank. He was short and dumpy with a dark complexion and a swarthy appearance. His eyes were shifty, and his black hair always looked unkempt and greasy. His clothes were sloppy and wrinkled.

Tory was a small guy; short and thin and scarce of hair. He had a pointed nose and beady eyes. Every time I looked at him he reminded me of Popeye. He liked to wear tight, white T-shirts and was always flexing his muscles. Tory was always nervous when Chuck was around. Chuck talked down to him and Tory's response was always to agree. For reasons we did not know, Tory was afraid of him. When Chuck came in with his girl, Tory said nothing even though Chuck was married to his daughter. It was a strange setup.

On one occasion I said, "These people live strange lives. Poor Tory, it must be embarrassing for him when Chuck brings Carole here. One wonders why he frequents our place."

"Sometimes you need to ignore what you don't like or what you see in the pub, Norma; not everyone lives as we do. Maybe Chuck and his wife have problems. We have never met her."

Frank and Tory were regular customers and fixtures in the bar. They never had much money. I was not happy with their choice. "Gosh Ben, was there no one else more suitable? Frank always looks so disgusting."

"Sorry, Norm, but we didn't have many choices on such short notice." He was irritated because I had promised not to lift anything heavy so soon after the baby.

After six weeks in traction, I was happy to be home. The children returned home and I was overwhelmed with joy, "God, how I've missed you." We hugged and hugged each other. They were happy to see me and vowed to help, which they did. They were good kids.

I spent time catching up on the books, realizing that no one had put in any entries. There were numerous discrepancies with the money and the cash register receipts.

I asked, "Has anyone checked to see if Frank has accounted for all the sales? It appears that the money and the receipts do not match." Ben and I went over the figures together and I explained the obvious entries I had put into the ledger. "Tomorrow, I am going to speak to Frank; I think he is stealing, what are your thoughts?"

Ben paused for a moment before he replied, "We have been busy and none of us took the time to check the receipts. Don't be too hasty, you are hardly back on your feet."

"Ben, stop trusting everyone so much. He is a shifty character and looks scruffy all the time. I hate seeing him behind our bar."

"Look", he said, "I know you don't like him, but let's go over this again. Perhaps there is an explanation." There was none.

The next day I wanted to speak to Frank, but the bar was busy and the opportunity did not present itself. That day, Ben came home in the afternoon, relieving Frank. "Hey," said Frank, "What are you doing home so soon?"

"We finished the job early, you can go home. I will take care of the bar."

Frank hesitated but removed himself reluctantly. He sat on a stool as a customer for a while, staring into space. Ben acknowledged his other customers, engaging in conversation. Frank finally left.

Underneath one of the liquor bottles, Ben found a $20 bill. The bill was folded nice and neat. "Look at this," he said to me.

"I hate to rub it in, but I told you so," I said. Frank was history. The next day, Ben stayed home. He decided to quit his job and waited for Frank to come in.

"Look, Frank, my job has ended and I am going to take over the bar. Norma is going to need my help, so I don't need you any more."

Frank was not pleased. He said, "Just like that."

"Yes," Ben replied, "Just like that. I am taking over the bar."

Frank mumbled to himself. "I guess that's me out of a job?" Ben did not respond. He knew Frank wanted long-term employment, but that was not going to happen regardless of the circumstances. This was probably the only job he'd had in a while. Frank glanced around, realized no one was concerned about him and decided to leave.

When Chuck came in that afternoon, he asked, "Where is Frank? I am surprised to see you behind the bar."

Ben replied, "I let him go. Frank is a good bartender, quick on his feet, and has the gift of the gab, but hiring him is like having another partner. Another partner I do not need. It was obvious Frank was working for himself. You know, one for me and one for you." Chuck said nothing and Ben continued, "Sorry to say, but your friend is a thief. Since you vouched for him, I wanted to tell you first."

Chuck was outraged. He sat at the bar quietly for a long period of time. His face was contorted and his eyes became small slits. "You're kidding," he said, "I didn't think he would do that. He and I need to have a conversation. I will take care of him. He knows better." Chuck had to know what Frank was. They had known each other for a long time. Frank was his father-in-law's best friend. How he would handle the situation, we did not know.

Ben remarked later, "You should have seen Chuck's face. He sat at the bar, swearing and talking to himself. If looks could kill, Frank would be dead. You know, I felt a chill run down my spine, he was so livid."

"I know what you mean. Once I saw him speaking to one of his friends. I caught him unaware and the hate in his eyes was scary, the guy looked terrified. Sometimes I wonder about him."

For several months, no one saw Frank. One day he reappeared as if nothing had happened. He had lost weight and sat quietly at the bar. He was no longer boisterous and it was obvious he was afraid of Chuck. It seemed Chuck had put him in his place.

We were once told that Frank was a small-time, petty crook.

According to Chuck, Frank had owned his own bar, but others disputed this and said he was only a manager of a pub. Rumor had it that he did not last long on the job. We also heard from customers that he had once worked for Sam DeStefano. They said Frank was a messenger boy. As time went by, we believed the source wanted to boost Frank's importance in our eyes. Chuck once told Ben, "Frank is a made man." The term made no sense to us. To us it was obvious that he was a dishonest and shifty character. He had embarrassed Chuck who wanted us to think he was a good guy.

CHAPTER 19: ENFORCING RULES

Chuck still worked on Friday nights, but Art was always around keeping an eye on things. We were weary of Chuck, but not sure how to handle the situation. He was not exactly the kind of guy one would just fire. We were afraid of the repercussions and decided to take it one day at a time. Maybe he would tire of the job or find another hangout. We began to realize that all the phone calls and whispering while at work was Chuck conducting business. What exactly Chuck's business involved was not clear, but we sensed it was not good. It seemed that with every passing day he was becoming more comfortable with his surroundings. He was trying to make himself indispensable.

One day he annoyed me as I worked behind the bar. The phone rang constantly and the calls were for him.

I said, "What's with all the phone calls. You need to tell your friends not to call you here all the time, if you don't mind. I am trying to wait on people and you are in my way. Besides, you are tying up the phone." Sensing my anger, he looked at me and apologized. He retreated to the other side of the bar and sat quietly as he watched me.

A few days later, he aired his complaints to Ben who listened carefully and sympathetically. "Well Chuck, it's Norma's place, too, and she makes most of the decisions. She feels the phone calls are not necessary, especially when you are not working. We have a business to run." Ben shrugged his shoulders. "You know how it is."

Chuck smiled a half smile. "Okay," he said. His lips formed a straight line. By this time, he was beginning to realize we were not too happy with him. The phone calls became less frequent. They were now coming in on the pay phone.

Art worried about the kids and me. Many times he would caution me, "You need to watch what you say around Chuck. He is not what he appears to be. Be careful. Somehow he is connected to the mob. Many times he acts like a gangster. One of my sons married a girl whose father was in the Syndicate. He was a gangster. My son and his wife were having problems. He wanted a divorce and one day he disappeared and I have not heard from him in several years." Art paused for a moment as if he was trying to compose himself. "I always run into stumbling blocks as I try to pursue it."

I saw tears in his eyes as he looked away from me. "What do you mean?" I asked.

"You don't want to know. Just be careful."

I smiled and touched his arm in a gesture of friendship and trust. "Yeah, I think I know what you are saying." I was not sure what he meant, but I could see he was upset. He never spoke of his first family very much. I did not want to pry into his personal life. I was glad he was around, especially when Ben was not here.

CHAPTER 20: AT A CROSSROADS

In the spring of 1964, we decided to put the business up for sale. The factory across the street had moved. Smaller factories moved in, but with lower wage workers. Our day trade was suffering. The bar was still busy, but the big spenders were gone. We continued to build up the night business, which became more chaotic each day. The pool table created many problems. Many men who were strangers came into our place. They were pool sharks and wanted to play pool for high stakes. Our customers were betting big money on these games. The losers were not very happy and fights would break out. Ben decided to put a stop to the gambling; this decision did not make him very popular.

There had been a lot of publicity about the robbery from the media and the story attracted people from near and far. There had been a few Irish folks that had come from the south side of Chicago. They had the same last name as us, but spelled differently. They were interested in meeting us and curious to see who we were. These folks were nice people and usually returned every weekend with several friends and enjoyed our place. Ben decided it was more fun having singsongs and customers dancing.

Ben said, "You know, Norma, this is a good time to sell while we can still attract a good crowd. I think we need to do something different."

We did not find many buyers; the ones that inquired either did not have any money or were illegal in the country. They would not qualify for a liquor license.

In the summer of July 1964, the stove factory closed. They moved their business down South where they were offered a lot of concessions and there were no unions. The factory area was renovated into smaller ones. Some new businesses had moved in while others were still under construction. Many of the construction workers who came into the bar were loud and boisterous, but the volume of people was not the same. The meals from the kitchen were far less and we decided to not cash checks anymore.

It became difficult working in the bar as the factories employed numerous workers who did not speak English. Most of the men spoke Spanish. We did our best, but it was hard to communicate. Ben did not encounter these men, as they were only day customers. With humor, Art and I did what we could with the language barrier.

CHAPTER 21: GOING HOME

It was hot and muggy in the summer of 1964. I felt irritated lately and wanted to go home to Canada. Having not been home for several years, I missed my family. It was a good time for a vacation. "Come with me, Ben, and meet the rest of my family. We could have some fun." He had never been to my hometown and I wanted him to see where I grew up.

Art was more than glad to help me and offered to watch the tavern while we were away. "You both need a rest," he said, "I will take care of everything." "Are you sure," asked Ben, "it's a big responsibility?"

Art's easy manner filled us with confidence. "Ben, I'm good. Have a nice time. Everything will be the same when you get back. Norma needs some time off. She works too hard. It is only for a short time."

Art insisted he had a friend who would help out, "I will take care of the business like it's my own. My friend is a good guy. I have known him for a long time and he's a nice man. He's the only person I trust, everything will be fine."

I hugged Art, "Thanks, you're my savior."

He winked at me, "I will even keep an eye on Chuck, okay." I squeezed his hand in appreciation. It was going to be an enjoyable couple of weeks away from the pub.

It was always nice to be home and feel the warmth and love of family. Watching the children with their grandparents and cousins warmed my heart. We were relaxed and enjoyed visiting with my brother Leo his wife Darlene and many of my friends that I grew up with. Leo took us to a few clubs where we had a wonderful time. Of course, Ben found a stage and gave us a song or two. They enjoyed his antics. In a conservative town such as Trail he was a breath of fresh air.

We also spent a few days with my sister Lillian and her husband Vic; they lived in Spokane, Washington. Vic was shy, but got along very well with Ben. Ben had a way of making people feel good. My brother Ron was unable to join us. He is a professor at Rice University in Houston, Texas and did not have the time off. We realized how time had passed and we had not spent much time with our parents. We promised ourselves things would change once we sold the tavern.

CHAPTER 22: MY TOWN

There is something unique about Trail and I would like to give everyone an insight into what a wonderful city it is. From where I lived in Warfield, one could walk to the end of the street and gaze down the mountain and see the city. Trail is situated deep in a gully with a beauty that is unsurpassed and unspoiled. The town is nestled in the Selkirk and Cascade Mountains, surrounded by beautiful, blue lakes, which reflect their grandeur. The rugged mountains surrounding the city reach great heights and are covered with snow peaks that I remember lasting all year round. The magnificent trees dressed the mountain like a blanket, concealing the secrets that were hidden in their splendor.

I can recall that if one shouted, the echo of your voice would shatter the silence. The mornings were always cool and crisp, a nip in the air, causing one to shiver. If you listened carefully you could hear the rustle of a small animal scampering into the trees. The sounds were so delightful to the ear. One could almost imagine the small animal pausing for a moment, listening to see if it were safe. Then it would perk up its ears to take in the silence of the dawn. It was magic.

Glancing down the rugged terrain, the pure beauty and untold mysteries filled your imagination. One could imagine fairies dancing under the streetlights. A blanket of fog covering the city and the lampposts looked like small dots. The huge mountains and tall, impressive trees clustered together forming large bouquets, coming together to form a natural wall protecting the city. Trail was such a contrast to Chicago. I smiled to myself and decided that today I would give Ben a tour of my city and its history.

I grew up in a small village called Warfield with approximately 2,000 residents. The houses were only 400 square feet, but built over two stories. Sometimes it was called Mickey Mouse town and I was never sure if it was because of the size of the homes or the fact it was inundated with mice.

I showed him where we skated every day and the mountains we climbed to ski. The old potbelly stove still stood in the shed where we used to warm our hands at the outdoor rink. Next door stood the garage where my brother Ron and I had the Sunshine Theater where we conducted plays each week for the neighborhood children. The old toboggan sled that Papa had constructed for us sat in the shed. I explained how we jumped on the sled with friends and raced down the mountain. Life was very simple then.

CHAPTER 23: THE SMELTER

As this was Ben's first visit to my town, I explained how Trail was the city of dreams for every person who hoped for a brighter future. Because it was once the fourth largest city in British Columbia, it presented many opportunities.

We drove past the Consolidated Mining and Smelter Company and once again my thoughts turned to my father. I pointed out to Ben the large buildings that harbored the smelter. If you looked to the left, you could see the large processing plants that sprawled over acres of land. Mostly everyone we knew worked there in one capacity or another. The smelter brought reassurance to the town and was the backbone of the city. It was a manufacturing plant that processed many different minerals and was built in 1895 to process ore such as lead and zinc. Gold and copper were found in the mountains and this created the beginning of our town.

We could see the smoke stacks looming large in the early morning light as if they were yawning to start a new day. Out of the stacks poured black smoke reaching far into the atmosphere. They created a trail of patterns that caressed the sky and then disappeared into the clouds over the mountaintop.

THE OLD HOUSE, WARFIEL

SMELTER, TRAIL, B.C.

TRAIL BY NIGHT   TRAIL, BRITISH COLUMBI

Remembering that Ben had been raised in Scotland during the Second World War from the time he was 9 to 14 years of age, I explained how the demand for ore was needed in large quantities to assist in the war effort. There were also rumors that the company was participating in the development of the atom bomb. I remember growing up and seeing the searchlight that circled around the valley and I never understood the significance of it. I now know the searchlight could detect any unidentified aircraft which entered the area.

We watched the Columbia River that ran through the center of the city. The white peaks that formed on the river roared like a lion forbidding anyone to enter the cold, murky, deep and mysterious waters. I pointed to the small vessels on the water that appeared similar to small dots being tossed around by the lion as they swayed in the breeze.

This was a city of numerous European immigrants. Countless Jewish families moved from the eastern part of Canada. The Chinese people were also a vital part of the community. Most of the Chinese were businessmen with restaurants, boarding houses and laundries. Men and women came from all walks of life for work and a fresh beginning. The educated as well as the common man who was willing to work hard came here. It was a very diverse community. It was ironic that Ben would meet someone he had gone to school with in my hometown.

Ben smiled at me as we finished touring the city, "It has almost as much history as my town in Scotland."

We enjoyed ourselves so much that we hated to go back to work and wished we could just stay a little longer. Mama seemed anxious when we left. She said, "I will miss the kids. I wish you could come home more often." I hugged her and replied, "I'll try." We flew back to Chicago to our little business. As much as we did enjoy our holiday, it was nice to be home again. Both of us missed home and worried about our pub.

CHAPTER 24: INTERROGATION

It was the end of July; a few weeks had passed since our vacation. The weather was still extremely hot, but business was brisk. The men poured into the bar for a couple of cold pints of beer. During lunch one day, I was clearing glasses off the tables when I glanced up and saw two well-dressed men in suits approach me. I wondered who they were. They were out of their element in this pub among blue-collar men in coveralls.

They flashed their badges, looked directly at me, and said, "Are you Norma McCluskie?" I replied that I was. "We are from the State's Attorney's Office and want to talk to you." I wondered what we had done. I asked Art to take over the bar and had Stacy leave the kitchen so we could have some privacy.

"What is this all about?" I asked in a friendly manner.

They were not so friendly. They got right into my face. I stepped back caught off guard at their tactics. They began firing a ton of questions at me.

"Tell us about the robbery. We know a great deal about the robbery. We know about the bribery and your relationship with Sam." I had a sinking feeling in my gut. I did not want to think about the robbery or Sam.

"We need some answers. We know everything about you, where you come from and know that you are here on a green card." They continued badgering me with threats of deportation. I stood silently and listened, saying very little. One officer said, "People with criminal records don't stay in this country." They were leveling all kinds of other threats such as jail time and closing the business.

In a gruff voice one of the officers said, "You'll have to come downtown with us and answer some questions." I was quite shaken, but was trying to portray some sense of dignity.

I asked, "Am I under arrest?" He shook his head. I responded, "Very well, but I need to take my car. One of you men can ride with me if necessary. I have to get back here. I have children; otherwise I need to make arrangements for them. Some are in school and some are upstairs." I looked at them and added, "Unless you plan to hold me once I get there?"

"We need to talk to you away from the noise here. We want answers to our questions. Of course the length of time depends on your answers." They looked at each other and nodded and one fellow got into my car with me. We drove in silence.

Thank God I wasn't handcuffed; it would have been embarrassing in front of my customers. Pausing on my way out, I spoke to Art briefly. He squeezed my hand. I felt more confident knowing he was in my corner. The questions resumed downtown at police headquarters. Most of the questions I answered, but I insisted that I could not identify the men because they wore masks.

I explained, "Mr. Santucci was pointed out to me in the lineup by the police officers. Otherwise, I could not have identified him."

When asked about Sam, I told them that he came into the bar on occasion, but that I did not know him personally. There were many questions they could have asked, but did not. I wondered why these questions were not asked, but felt grateful because I would not be able to answer them truthfully. The questions would have been about the visit to Sam's home. They did not push the issue. They were holding back information for reasons I did not understand and were nicer to me downtown.

CHAPTER 25: PORTRAIT OF A KILLER

That day changed my life. The officers from the State's Attorney's Office left me sitting in a room with a long table and chairs placed around it. I was nervous, but sat quietly, many thoughts running through my head. Soon, two different men came in and sat across the table from me. The older agent was a short, squat man with a cynical attitude. He had a folder or portfolio in his hand.

He started by saying, "Look, I am going to show you what kind of people you are dealing with. You have no idea about these men and we are worried about you and your family." His voice was firm, even though he seemed irritated.

He studied me for a few minutes before he spoke again. "I am sure you do not know very much about Sam DeStefano and I want to give you an insight to the kind of person he really is. There is much more than what is in these folders." He picked up the folders and waved them around. Choosing his words carefully, he continued, "Sam is known as the worst torturer of any individual in the United States. He is not a nice person and is a man to be afraid of. In these folders you will read of the crimes he has committed and the kind of character he is. In his home he has a soundproof basement where he has killed and tortured many men. Sam is mentally unstable."

He had my attention. I stared at him, unsure if his words were registering correctly. Was he trying to scare me?

He handed me the folder. I sat for a moment and stared at it. I was afraid to open it, as I feared its contents. As I read the criminal record of Sam DeStefano, my eyes were really opened. There was a massive amount of information written about him. My stomach was in knots as I tried to digest what was documented. I felt fearful about our situation.

In September of 1955, it had been alleged that Sam had shot and killed his own brother, Michael, who was a drug addict. He put him in the trunk of his car. Allegedly, he later notified the police with an anonymous phone call about Mike's whereabouts, but it had never been proven that he made the call.

The officer watched me and then interrupted, "Sam was questioned about his brother, and we believe he was ordered to take Mike out. He was becoming a nuisance and the Syndicate wanted rid of him. When we spoke to Sam about this incident in court, he laughed. Unfortunately we have been unable to prove it yet."

The officer continued, "In 1961, Sam was involved in the murder of William Jackson. Jackson was a large man and weighed over 300 pounds. He was also a collector for some unscrupulous loans. It has been alleged that Jackson was killed in the basement of DeStefano's home. Jackson was hung up on a meat hook, where he was shot, tortured, and beaten. He was stripped naked. This guy died a horrible death. The torture they used was indescribable." He did not want to tell me how he was tortured. I read later that they used a blowtorch, a cattle prod and an ice pick. Because he was a big man, a truck was used to haul his body and dump it on the side of a road. He had suffered for several days before his life ended.

"We have been unable to pin it on Sam. We have informants, but we need the proof." He paused for a moment, "It is also alleged that Crimaldi was present and participated in this murder. I could tell you many stories about Sam, most are unpleasant. I know this is probably shocking to you, but you need to know about Sam. His wife Anita is terrified of him and he often beats her. He has threatened to kill her. Once again, I want you to know this is the kind of guy we are dealing with. Look, I will let you read his file and then we can discuss anything you want." I tried to keep my emotions from registering on my face. I lowered my head then began to read the rest of the file.

CHAPTER 26: SAM'S RAP SHEET

The court documents revealed that Sam's criminal record began in 1926. He had at least 40 arrests for crimes including assault with a deadly weapon, burglary, contempt of court, bribery and intimidation of a Federal Judge. He was also a suspect in the bombing of several restaurants. Sam was also cited for connections to six other murders that could not be proven. There were many articles written about his crimes, each one appearing worse than the last.

Sam was accused of rape more than once. He was convicted on one of the rape charges and received a three-year prison sentence. His toughest sentence was when he was found guilty of bank robbery. For this, he served 11 years in State Prison at Waupun, Wisconsin.

His convictions also included possession of illegal sugar stamps for which he served one year and one day. For an assault with a deadly weapon, Sam received a fine of $200. He was also cited for contempt of court several times, once receiving thirty days and fined for the other times. For the conviction of illegal voting, he received one to three years, which was reversed on appeal.

"Sam was smart," said the older agent. "In the years he spent in prison, he read many books and educated himself. He used his time in prison to learn how to defend himself in the courts as his own consul. The State Penitentiary where he served his time was a prison where the prisoners were prohibited to speak. They were kept in silence most of the time. He took advantage of this."

He watched me read a few more pages, and then said, "Sam

DeStefano likes to think of himself as a businessman. In reality, he is a loan shark, a Mafia mobster or you can say he is in the juice loan racket business. He loans money to persons who cannot or do not want to obtain legal loans. He charges extortionate interest rates and penalties that are not sustainable. He uses men like Chuck Crimaldi to collect these loans. They use some pretty treacherous methods to do so."

"Neither Sam nor Chuck are nice people. Both delight in hurting people. They have no regard for human life. There are many stories about Sam DeStefano and they do not paint a pretty picture."

He continued, "These guys are animals. Sam's nickname is 'The Mad Hatter of the Crime Syndicate.' Many people call him crazy. He is sadistic and tortures people for pleasure. He is a sexual psychopath, and a guy once told me once he worships the devil. To tell you the truth, he is borderline insane and Chuck is not much different. Chuck does whatever Sam tells him to do. When Sam says jump, you jump. Chuck tortures people as well." I thought about the devil worship. The sight of Sam's face flashed through my mind. It was a night I will never forget.

The older officer paused for a few seconds. "Maybe this is hard for you to understand because you do not encounter people like this. But in the case of Santucci and company, Sam has an investment in them. They have to continue to steal to pay off loans they obtained from Sam. They use the money for bail and court costs, which Sam provides to keep them out of jail." He paused.

"There is no excuse for them because they wanted easy money without working. Because Sam continues to finance Santucci, he has never spent a day in jail. He has been accused of committing many robberies and other crimes, but he always managed to escape doing time. He continually gets away with his crimes. Sam and Santucci both need to be taken off the streets."

The officer paused once again to allow me to digest all this information. Before he left he said, "I am not trying to scare you.

Also, I am not being hard, but this is serious business. You need to take it seriously. I will leave you now because there is a lot of reading there."

The younger officer who had not spoken in all this time said, "I will be back shortly, please think about the information given to you." Somehow it did not seem real.

It took me some time to read about Sam. I was truly upset and cannot describe the sick feeling I had. I remembered once Ben told me that while Sam was in the pub having a drink, a customer began to harass him. He did not know what had been said but the customer ran out of the pub with Sam in pursuit. Sam jumped into his car and chased the fellow down Albany Avenue towards the pub on the corner. Sam wheeled the car onto the sidewalk as he tried to run the guy over. The man jumped over a fence and disappeared into the night. Sam came back to the pub cursing and swearing.

A customer said to Ben, "That Sam guy tried to run him over." No one gave up the man's name and claimed he was a stranger to the pub.

Only the younger officer returned. He had brought me some coffee and doughnuts. "I thought you might be hungry." He sat down facing me at the table and we drank our coffee in silence. "Now it's my turn; I need to tell you about Chuck."

CHAPTER 27: CHUCK UNVEILED

The young State's Attorney's agent gave me some background on Chuck. He said, "There is not a lot written about him in our files but enough to know he works for Sam. We do not have a lot of information on record about Crimaldi. Most of what we do have came from one of the police precincts. They had a pretty good file on him. We had to request it. The police department was reluctant to give it up."

The agent explained, "Chuck is what is called the collector. His job is to cater to every one of Sam's whims. He makes sure anyone who borrows money from Sam is responsible and pays on time. Sam has many rules. Chuck enforces them. If a man is late with a payment, we are told Chuck will hunt him down and tell him in no uncertain terms that he is late with his payment. A few whacks with a baseball bat on the knees usually gets their attention. At first these are friendly, but if the guy made him angry he would break his kneecaps. Chuck is sadistic and he loves the power over another man."

The officer looked at me before continuing, "Chuck's favorite weapons are the baseball bat or a .38-caliber pistol. Believe me; he is good at his job. Also, to him it is just that, a job. I want you to know his title is hitman." He paused then continued, "You know what a hitman is, don't you?"

"Yes," I replied, "it's someone hired to kill another person." I looked at him, remembering the gun and the baseball bat. The officer smiled at me, he was nice, young and handsome. I knew he was trying to gain my confidence.

He said, "I met one of the police officers from the precinct who knows Chuck well and he was willing to talk off the record. This police officer is what we call an informant. I invited the police officer to come with me to an undisclosed location where we could talk. I said to him. Let's have a cup of coffee. I need some information about Crimaldi."

He continued, "This police officer told me they both grew up near an area called The Patch, which was not far from Albany Avenue and he knew where Chuck lived. He said, 'Did you know Chuck has a bartending job on Albany Avenue at one of the small taverns? I have been there and many of his cronies go there.' Anyway, I decided not to respond to this, as I did not want to give my hand away. I just wanted to get some information about Chuck and his connection with Sam."

"Well, apparently Norma, this policeman and Chuck went to the same school. He said Chuck's mother was a widow and his father had died when he was very young. He had several brothers and sisters. He hung around with his brother Tony most of the time. He was always in trouble from an early age. I think he was about eight when he was first busted for burglary. Chuck spent a lot of time in juvenile hall. He was a pretty cocky kid."

Their folder on Chuck was quite small. Most of what I learned about him that day was related verbally. He claimed Chuck Crimaldi was bad from an early age and as a teenager he progressed to bigger crimes with his brother Tony. I was told the brothers adored each other.

Chuck's rap sheet stated how he served time in Pontiac State Penitentiary for burglary and for violating his probation for armed robbery. This penitentiary catered to younger boys under twenty. The prison had a program where they tried to offer trades and a different way of life to the young men. Sometimes they were successful, other times unsuccessful. Chuck received a trade as a plumber.

Chuck was about sixteen when he was sent to prison, sometime in the late forties or early fifties. He received a sentence that was to last from four to ten years. He was released from prison around 1954, when he was approximately twenty-one years old. According to the documents, it seemed he spent just over four and a half years in prison.

After allowing me to read for a few minutes, the agent continued to share information about Chuck's relationship with Sam. "Sam heard about Chuck from other criminals he knew. Chuck was a repeat offender. Because of his repeat offenses, he was tried in an adult court and sent to prison. Sam scours the jails for guys who need help and whom he thinks could be useful to him. Sam employs many collectors; Chuck is just one of them. He heard about Chuck through his crimes and reputation. Chuck's mother coming to Sam was a bonus. She knew him from the neighborhood and thought he may help Chuck get a job upon his release. He played on her trust and took over the role of a father figure. My informant told me that Sam even approached *him* once, but he was not interested."

I continued to listen in silence. "Sam went to see Chuck any chance he could. His visits were usually when Chuck's mother was not around. He began teaching Chuck many ways of how to be a good criminal. He was also instructing Chuck how to create havoc in the prison. Sam's purpose was to educate Chuck of how to be callous and learn the skills to become a hitman. Sam promised him he would try and get him an early release. He also promised him a job when he came out of prison. Sam was unable to pull any strings on an early release for Chuck. He did serve in excess of four years, but this was better than the ten he could have spent in the penitentiary. There was a job for him when he was released from prison. That promise Sam was able to keep."

I shifted uncomfortably in my seat as Chuck's story continued to unfold. "When Chuck was released from prison, he discovered his brother Tony was badly hooked on heroin. You know heroin is a powerful drug. Chuck knew about drugs from the prison and was shocked. He once told my informant that Tony and he had big plans but his big plans disappeared. Chuck tried to help Tony, but he was a helpless case. One night Chuck was so angry about what happened to Tony, he swore he would kill every drug dealer in town."

"Sam has many connections with politicians, policemen and attorneys as well as judges who look the other way to help guard his fraudulent business. Sam can afford to pay off these officials. Many of the court cases that were due to be heard in the courts were discussed and solved at Sam's home on Sayre Avenue. He got people to change their testimony; this is how most of the criminals associated with Sam manage to escape prosecution."

I was certain I had been sitting there for hours, but the agent continued to speak: "The police officer told me he had been at Sam's home. You would not believe what goes on there. A lot of people will do anything for money. Do you know how many of these high officials need money for gambling or girlfriends? Sam gets them hooked and they never get away from his clutches. He uses these guys, which is why he is able to operate so openly." He paused, "These small-time crooks are free to hurt other people and get away with it. By the way," he said matter-of-factly, "Chuck is always there at Sam's house.

"Would you like another cup of coffee?" he asked with a smile. "In the next few minutes I am going to wrap up this discussion and you need to go home. I want you to think and discuss with your husband all the information we have given you today. Then we will talk again."

He stopped, and then brought me another cup of coffee. When he returned, he sat down and said in earnest, "Chuck has no conscience and is as ruthless as Sam. In his world, everyone and everything is disposable. He is loyal to Sam and Sam trusts him. The police officer also told me that Chuck is now Sam's favorite hitman and Chuck will do anything he wants him to do. You need to part company with him as your family is not safe with him around.

Someone is going to get hurt. The officer also told me that Crimaldi likes to boast about the men he has killed. He claims they deserved to die. I believe he has a twisted sense of reality."

He went on, "The informer laughed when he told me it wasn't hard getting information; Chuck liked to brag about all the hits he did. Crimaldi started out with Sam on a part-time basis. Chuck told the informer that he wasn't sure what he wanted to do but Sam began to rely on him more and more. Sam was always testing his loyalty and Chuck passed with flying colors. My informant recalls Chuck saying, 'I just follow Sam's instructions to the letter. I never ask a lot of questions. Sam is like a father to me.'"

The State's Attorney's officer looked at me and said, "Chuck believes Sam trusts him but Sam trusts no one." He paused, "There is nothing he will not do for Sam. He likes to feel important. Think about what I am saying and you need to be careful."

The other information I got that day from the agent was that Chuck was not receiving the kind of money he felt he deserved. The officer had told him, "Even though Chuck works for Sam, he is still robbing other places. He likes to live the high life and always needs money. I knew a couple of guys that went out with him on some robberies. They said Chuck was always real cool. He was not afraid to smack the guy around with his gun. This is Chuck Crimaldi as I know him"

The agent handed me his card, "Look, if you need to know anything or ask a question, call me."

CHAPTER 28: DECISIONS

These conversations replayed over and over in my mind as I drove home. "How did we get ourselves in such a position? Was Chuck this murderer who had no regard for people? Was he as sadistic as the officer said? Somehow I believed the story about Sam because so much was documented but I couldn't get my head around what I'd heard about Chuck. Could he really be a killer? Was he a hitman? We knew Chuck had a nasty and violent side. He did hide that side of his personality very well. Could we have been so wrong? As I thought back, I realized there were signs, but we had ignored them. So many things began to fall into place: the phone calls, the baseball bat, the gun. I could go on and realized we had been surrounded by evil. I shuddered, "God, how we trusted him."

I thought about the time he brought his mother to the pub. He introduced us to her. She was a nice lady. I remembered how attentive he was as he hovered over her. There was the time when Ben brought him a gift from Scotland. He was in awe and wore the sweater proudly.

I was gone for over four hours. It was getting dark. The streets were busy with commuters coming home from work. I knew Art would see that the children were all right. He would explain to Ben what had happened. I worried all the way home. I was afraid, afraid of the police and afraid of Sam. I tried to digest what I read and what I had been told. Nothing seemed real. Chuck, a murderer? What would have been our fate if we had not taken the bribe? Would Chuck have whacked us?

The feeling in my stomach grew like an abscess. Ben and I had to discuss this turn of events. We had to decide what the best option available to us was. I wondered what Chuck would say. Surely he would realize that I had heard the awful details of his crimes. I also needed to call our ex-partners and explain to them what had happened. There had to be a decision as to what we were going to do. They were involved as much as we were.

Apparently, the State's Attorney's officers had also gone to our ex partners home at the same time they were interrogating me. There had to be a solution where everyone would be safe. In the end we decided to tell the truth. Ret would testify before a Grand Jury. She would testify that she had lied on the witness stand in the robbery trial. In addition she would testify that several weeks after she identified Robert Chesser's photo, Sam DeStefano had contacted us and offered us a bribe.

CHAPTER 29: FACING REALITIES

When I arrived home I could see Ben and Art were worried about me. Ben said, "You were gone a long time."

I replied, "I know, I'll tell you about it later." I was not ready to talk about my afternoon; there was so much to think about. I wanted to speak to Ben before I said anything to Art.

Later that night after the bar was closed. Ben and I sat upstairs and talked far into the night. I told him all that had happened at the Attorney's office. He said, "I wish I had been there with you. I hate to think you were being interrogated for all that time."

"Actually," I replied, "it was not like an interrogation, it was like a story they wanted to tell me. I just listened. I was scared."

When Ben heard all the accounts about Sam and Chuck, he felt betrayed. He said, "I knew Sam was something evil, I heard a lot about him. Many people were scared of him. That night at his house is something I won't forget." He continued, "I was aware that Chuck had more going on that he let on. A lot of the guys said he was a gangster, but killing people! God Norma, it is hard to believe he kills people on such a large scale and gets away with it."

Ben's eyes reflected his confusion as he said, "I have spent a lot of time with Chuck. He has a violent side to him but fighting and killing are two different things. I knew he could be nasty and after that incident with Bobby I never trusted him. There's something deceitful and dishonest about him, but you know he has always been okay with us. Do you think he's stolen anything from us?"

"No Ben, I think that way he's okay, but he uses our place to conduct his business."

"Many times he has spoken about trying to straighten out his life. He seemed to be in a rut, but never disclosed what he wanted to change. You know me I always give someone a chance. I just can't believe he is a murderer. I know he is capable of killing someone but to do this for money just blows my mind. God, can you imagine hitting a guy with a baseball bat, it is bad enough to hurt them. He would have done that to Bobby if I had not stopped him. To take it as far as to kill someone is worse. I can't understand people like that. He certainly had me fooled." He put his head in his hands.

"In Scotland we had fist fights and wanted to win. We really did not want to hurt the other guy. Some guys were treacherous; they would give you a head butt but not to kill you."

I looked at him and suddenly I was angry, "You spent so much time with him, what in God's name did you talk about?"

Ben also became angry, "We talked about jobs, women, music, night clubs, and we certainly did not talk about killing people. What the hell do you think we talked about?"

I replied quietly, "I don't know Ben; I only know that this guy has been with us for nearly four years and apparently we did not know a thing about him. We trusted him, he played with our children, you socialized with him and we didn't even know him. The stuff I have read and heard about him, it's scary."

Both of us were distraught. This level of violence was something we did not understand. We talked about it frequently in the days that followed. Becoming more aware of our surroundings, we began watching people with suspicion. I know Ben felt betrayed because he had befriended Chuck to the extent that he had. He was always too trusting. Usually he was a good judge of character but had been fooled. Ben said,

"You were always wary of him. You are a better judge of

character than I am." He rarely admitted he was wrong. There was no need to respond. Chuck was smooth and calculating.

CHAPTER 30: CHANGES

When Chuck came into work the following Friday, I looked at him as if I was seeing him for the first time. He greeted many customers as he made his way behind the bar. He smiled at me and my stomach felt sick. I tried to relate the stories the agent revealed to me to the Chuck we knew. We felt used and were angry with ourselves. We had to be careful of what we said and pretend we knew nothing more about him than he wished to portray to us.

We were very conscious that Chuck would be upset when we told him what had happened. Both Ben and I felt we needed to tell him about the State's Attorney's office because we knew he would find out from another source. Knowing what he was capable of, we felt we had to protect ourselves and I know we both wanted him gone.

It was not what he said, but the expression on his face that spoke volumes. "When did this all go down?" he questioned. His voice was strained.

My heart was pounding. I could not look at him. I replied quietly, "On Tuesday, through the week. Remember, we have not seen you since last weekend.

They also stopped at Ret's and Packy's home. All of us came to the same conclusion. "We need to tell the truth. You know we do not have many choices."

His face was ashen. "I need to let Sam know what is going on." A few days later, Chuck decided he could no longer work for us. He called Ben to the end of the bar, "I need to speak to you, it's important. You know I can no longer work here. I have to take sides. I wish this had never happened, but Sam will expect me to be there with him. You know this involves me as well."

Ben responded, "Sorry, Chuck, I understand. I am taking sides too."

He reached out and shook Chuck's hand, "No hard feelings."

"No hard feelings."

We were thankful he was gone, but at the same time apprehensive. It was something we had hoped for, but we suddenly felt uncertain about the situation. He seemed to be sorry he was leaving; I believe he genuinely liked us.

Ben said he felt relieved and was glad he was gone, but he was worried. He said, "We are in a real mess. I can't believe all we are hearing and seeing. It is funny you see things and you let them pass. I am not sure what is going to happen now. More than ever we need to be on our guard."

Ben befriended a chap from Tennessee, James C Pugh. J.C. was his nickname. He had frequented the pub for some time. It had not gone unnoticed how much admiration he received from his friends. He came from a small town in Tennessee called Covington. J.C. was a tall man who stood well over six feet. He had dark eyes, jet-black hair and a mild manner. He commanded respect amongst his peers. If there was a dispute in the bar, it was quickly settled, without any violence. He would speak to the persons involved in his quiet manner and the problem was solved.

Ben realized J.C. had lost his job and was unemployed. He decided to speak to some of the men he knew at Midwest Fence. This was a thriving company that installed fences along the expressways. After Ben had spoken to his friends, J.C. got the job. It was a good job and he was very grateful.

With the departure of Chuck, many of his colleagues disappeared and a new batch of night customers emerged. The changing neighborhood was attracting many people from the southern states such as Kentucky, Tennessee, and Mississippi, North and South Carolina and many others. Many of the Polish and Italian folks who owned homes in the area were moving to the suburbs. If they could not sell their homes, they were renting and to afford the rent, more than one family would move in together.

We decided to hire J.C. as our Friday night bartender. He eagerly accepted the job. The pub was his social life. Since most of the customers were from the South, he seemed to bond with them.

The Southerners were passionate people who loved to have fun. They loved their music and the jukebox and were skillful on the pool table. J.C. was honest, reliable and possessed many wonderful qualities; above all, he was sincere. He was married with two children, a boy and a girl who were the same ages as our two boys. Ben also blended in well with the new clientele. They all had names that implied their ancestors came from Scotland or Ireland. He felt akin to them.

CHAPTER 31: STOOL PIGEON

Much of the information that the State's Attorney's office relayed to me came from a small-time hood, Vito Zaccagnini. He was under arrest and placed under guard in the witness quarters of the Cook County jail. Vito was hooked on a $3,000 loan he received from DeStefano, which he could not pay; the amount doubled and tripled by penalties and became a debt of $28,000. DeStefano said Vito had to steal if necessary to pay his debt or he would kill him. Because of this situation, Vito talked to the FBI. He was looking for help to try and save himself, knowing what the consequences would be.

I remember this guy, Vito. He came to the pub once with Stefano and stood behind him. At the time I did not pay attention, but thought he acted like a bodyguard. I rarely spoke to Sam, keeping my distance. At that time, Chuck still worked Friday nights. On this occasion, Sam had come to the tavern buying drinks for everyone, letting his presence be known. This was the first we had seen of him since the court case. He had won a victory with the courts and was pleased, "Give the bar a drink, come on everyone have a drink," he shouted as he threw a hundred-dollar bill on the counter. Most men did not earn that much money in a week. Always the big shot, but this time he was gloating. He had succeeded in scaring us enough to comply with his tactics, setting his robber friends free. Chuck had seemed embarrassed.

Zaccagnini had many interviews with Capt. William Duffy, head of the Intelligence department. At one point I was told, "We asked him about the robbery case on Albany Avenue and asked him if it was fixed. Vito took a deep breath and said, "You are right, Sam fixed it."

CHAPTER 32: PERJURIES

In September 1964, the State's Attorney's Office charged Sam with conspiracy to commit perjury. The hearing was set for September 21, 1964. Because of Chuck's role as the person who connected us with Sam, they charged him with conspiracy to bribe. The success of the prosecution depended on our testimony. Sam was the big prize that the Attorney's Office wanted. I was told it was an election year and the conviction of anyone connected to the Mafia was a bonus for their office. The public would be impressed if they were to secure the conviction of a known gangster, especially someone like Sam who was never out of the news.

Because we would have to testify, I was worried for the safety of my children. Shortly after my visit from the State's Attorney's officers, sometime in August 1964, Sam came to the pub and wanted to speak to us in private. He had one of his daughters with him. He spoke to Ben first, but insisted that he also had to speak to me. Ben brought him into the kitchen downstairs and called me down from our apartment. I came down and stood on the landing. I did not want him coming upstairs into my home. I looked down at him standing there. After all I read about him, I knew he was a sick human being.

"What do you want?" The tone of my voice was sharp. Sam ignored my tone, glanced up and smiled at me, "We are friends," he said warmly. "I have a family and need to take care of them, you understand that. You have family. We love our families. These guys are always after me. They blame me for everything and they will make me do time. My family needs me. Who will help take care of my children?" He looked up at me, took off his glasses and pleaded. I felt cold and unresponsive.

I looked at the little girl. She was about ten years old. She was uncomfortable standing there, not knowing where to look. I thought, *Why did you bring this child with you?*

He continued, "Look, you cannot testify against me. I helped you out. I didn't have to, but I did. You should know I am your friend. Now I need you to help me out." He paused, "Everyone blames me for everything. Blame Sam, he's got broad shoulders. Why not blame Sam." He waved his arms around. He was whining and looked pathetic. "I am a man you can trust. I help lots of people like I helped you. When I gave my word I delivered, I have principles."

I felt sorry for the little girl as she watched her father beg. Sam liked everyone to believe he had this code of ethics and his word was his bond. He expected the same in return. Suddenly the tone of his voice changed and he became arrogant and derogatory, "Why do you stay in this stinking place. I can offer you a classy place on the strip. It is a nice area and good for the kids." He snickered, "This is a terrible place for your family among these low-life people. I offer prestige." The strip was where all the high-class nightclubs were located on Mannheim Road. Ben politely said thanks, but no thanks. We were not ready for that type of move.

"Think about it." Sam said. "You need a nice place for your family. Family is everything. You help me, I will help you. I can get you a wonderful place for your family away from this scum."

"Thanks," replied Ben, "but we like our own place."

"You need to think about it seriously, where you bring up your family is important."

I listened as long as was possible then blurted, "I can't help you." I turned quickly and hurried up the stairs. There was nothing to say or think about.

He stood there for several minutes then turned to Ben, "She needs to think about this and not be so hasty. I am asking for a small favor. You need to talk to her. Bad things can happen."

After he left, Ben came upstairs. He said, "I am concerned. I will stand by you, Norma, whatever you decide to do. I'm here to support you. I know you're scared and know how you feel about him. I feel the same way. He is a dangerous person, but I am worried. These people are nuts."

I replied angrily, "I loathe him. He is an arrogant son of a bitch and I don't want to talk about him anymore." I started to cry.

"It's one thing testifying against a couple of low-class robbers, but Sam has a lot of connections. I hope we are doing the right thing," he said quietly.

"I don't know Ben; it is not up to me. According to the State's Attorney's Office, Ret will be doing most of the testifying. He should be talking to her. All I can testify to is that we were present when he offered the bribe. Remember, Packy picked up the money from Sam's house and put it in the cashbox. I am scared and worried; I just have to hope everything will come out okay. There is nothing I can do. It is out of my hands."

Ben said later. "Sam is not going to own us, I know what he is. His proposition about a nightclub, can you imagine what kind of life we would have?"

CHICAGO SUN-TIMES, Wed., Jan. 13, 1965

Debtor Rebels; DeStefano Guilty

By Sandy Smith

Sam De Stefano, 55, Cosa Nostra loan shark, was convicted Tuesday in a case exposed by a borrower he had threatened to murder.

A Criminal Court jury found De Stefano guilty of conspiracy to commit perjury after deliberating one hour, 45 minutes. Police later in the day told how the borrower, terrorized by De Stefano's death threats and demands for "juice" (exorbitant interest), had revealed De Stefano as a payoff man and fixer.

It was disclosed that three law enforcement agencies—the Federal Bureau of Investigation, the police Intelligence Division and the state's attorney's office — worked to-

gether to protect the borrower and convict De Stefano.

The Sun-Times learned that the perjury conviction resulted from the story told by Vito Zaccagnini, now under guard in the witness quarters of the Cook County Jail.

The 38-year-old Zaccagnini reported that he was hooked on a $3,000 loan from DeStefano three years ago.

But his "juice" bill doubled and tripled by "penalties" assessed by DeStefano for various reasons. It was his plea for more time to pay that caused DeStefano to threaten his life.

To make him pay, Zaccagnini related, DeStefano forced him to steal and threatened to kill him.

According to Intelligence

Division detectives, it was De Stefano's terrorism, along with the possibility of prosecution for the crimes he had committed to pay "juice," that impelled Zaccagnini to tell first to the FBI.

Later, when Zaccagnini involved DeStefano in state law violations, the FBI brought the Intelligence Division into the case.

Months ago, Zaccagnini explained to the Intelligence...

...and later state's attorney's men. They have to steal just to pay juice to DeStefano. It will stop — a lot of crime if DeStefano is convicted and sent to prison.

In the case built on Zaccagnini's tip, a ring of eight men and four women convicted DeStefano of arranging a $1,000 payoff in a state's witness in a 1962 holdup case.

DeStefano could be sentenced to five years in prison. The four short has been imprisoned three times, for bank robbery, black marketing and rape. He now is serving a unexpected term in the Cook County Jail for contempt of court.

The Criminal Court room of

Judge George N. Leighton was locked and ringed by extra guards Tuesday when the jurors brought in the guilty verdict in the perjury case.

DeStefano heard the verdict, however, without the outbursts of defiance that had landed him in the County Jail for contempt of court.

The jury found DeStefano guilty of giving $1,000 to the operators of a tavern at 718 N. Albany so they would not identify three men who robbed him in 1962. The bandits subsequently were acquitted.

With the conviction of De Stefano, Capt. William Duffy, commander of the Intelligence Division, took the wraps off mercy of the case and the disclosures of Zaccagnini.

When the FBI made him available to the Intelligence Division almost a year ago, Zaccagnini talked cautiously, Duffy said.

But a veteran detective, in the course of many patient interviews, gained Zaccagnini's confidence.

"Finally Zaccagnini showed that he trusted us to protect his life," Duffy said. "We asked

While the De Stefano verdict is being read, courtroom doors are locked (above) as precaution against outburst. (Sun-Times Photo)

him about reports we had heard that the robbery case was fixed. Vito took a deep breath and said 'Yes, it right.'—Sun fixed it'"

...in Koulkpia in police ...tody at Gardena, Calif. ...)

CHAPTER 33: STATE'S ATTORNEY

A few days after Sam's visit, the threatening phone calls started. They came in the mornings and evenings. These calls put me on edge. They were effective. I was paranoid and began making phone calls to Ret from a pay phone. I believed that our phone was tapped. My first priority was to call my mother so that I could explain what was going on. I also had to tell her that I would like to send the children to Canada. I needed her to take care of them for me, as I was fearful for their safety. My mother listened carefully to me. I knew she was crying softly and so was I.

She said quietly, "I agree with you and it is all right. I will be happy to have them. Please, take care of yourself."

My next decision was that I must have a talk with the State's Attorney's Office. This panicky feeling in my gut told me something was not right. I could not put my finger on my predicament, but had a premonition that things were beyond my control. Sam's visit had unnerved me more than I had let on. I was scared. Sam was a desperate man. I asked myself, "Did I handle his visit correctly. What else could I have done?" There were no answers. I put on a brave face, but did not feel very courageous.

I cannot remember which of the men I spoke to. It was a long time ago, but I feel fairly certain that I spoke to U.S. Attorney Edward Hanrahan. Other men in charge at this office were the State's Attorney, who at this time was Daniel P. Ward, and his first assistant, Edward Egan. Whoever the official was, he seemed too busy to talk to me and let me sit in this office the entire day. He finally agreed to see me because his secretary, who was about to leave, informed him I was still in the waiting room. It troubled me that this office would receive what they wanted by getting a conviction of a man they had been after for years. I felt as if we were being ignored as they disregarded any concern for our safety. His attitude was beginning to piss me off. This conviction was more about politics and getting a promotion. There were no concerns of justice or protection of a witness.

It was obvious he was not pleased that I was there. By now, I was angry at being treated in this shabby manner and let him know it. I felt ill at ease. He shuffled some papers on his desk as if he were preoccupied. There was not a chance that I would leave until I had spoken to someone. I needed to explain about the phone calls and how I feared for my children's safety.

He was an arrogant man and his clipped voice barely concealed his annoyance. "What can I do for you? This is a busy office. Sorry I kept you waiting."

I replied, "Yes I know. I am busy, too, but I need to talk to you. I have sat in this office all day and I also have a family to take care of." I paused, "My time is precious, too. I am here to discuss many things that are bothering me. Let me tell you about the phone calls and Sam's visit. I am scared for my children and have thought about sending them to my parents." I explained everything to him. He kept his head bowed and stared at his desk. I was becoming increasingly anxious as I spoke, "I'm scared." I could feel the tears well up in my eyes. I felt so small and insignificant.

He stared at me, for a few minutes before he replied. "I think you are being paranoid and silly. There are many things these gangsters do, but they have never been known to harm children."

Our conversation continued, "I can't help it. I am petrified of something terrible happening to my family. After reading all that material you have in your office about these gangsters, I feel that they will stop at nothing. They are desperate people."

He sat quietly as he looked at me. Then he spoke in a kinder and gentler voice. "Look," he said, "I will have police guards placed at your place of business. There will be a guard in the front and one at the back of the tavern. If it makes you feel better, I will assign a guard to go to work with your husband. Also I shall assign a guard to go to school with your children. You will be well protected." He paused, "I don't believe all this is really necessary, but if it makes you feel better consider it done."

He made me feel foolish. I felt a little better, but still was apprehensive. I really did not want my children to be so far away from me. My mother would understand when I told her.

Perhaps I was being paranoid.

I should have followed my instincts. My gut feeling was to put the children out of harm's way, but they had been so clingy, lately. I was reluctant to let them go and convinced myself that I would feel better having the guards.

I called my mother to tell her. "Are you sure?" she asked.

"I think they will be okay, I worry too much." I tried to keep my voice light, "The guards will make a difference. I feel safer, now." I was trying to convince myself as well as her.

CHAPTER 34: GUARDS

The guards were posted the next day. There was one guard posted at the back of the tavern in the alley and another in the front of the tavern. The guard in the front of the tavern was James Daniels. Our ex-partners also had guards at their home. Ret received officers from the State's Attorney's Office as guards. We received police officers from the task force. Ret would be the obvious target, as it would be her testimony which would convict Sam. She could tie Robert Chesser to the holdup, which in turn incriminated Sam for the bribe.

When I spoke to Ret on the phone, I somehow got the impression they were sitting in her house having tea. I could hear the guards laughing in the background. I felt annoyed. Ret was baring her soul to these guys and we were sitting ducks. In my heart I felt we were most vulnerable as we were in a public place where people came and went all day.

I had been on edge all week and said to Ben, "We are a target, here; anyone can walk into the tavern. We wouldn't know who he or she was." I could see he was worried and had also thought about our safety.

He answered me with a sigh, "I know, Norma, but we have to trust someone. I hope these guards know what they are doing. Let's try not to worry." He squeezed my hand and hugged me.

The trial was scheduled for the end of September 1964. Everything that was discussed behind closed doors in the State's

Attorney's Office was relayed back to me in the threatening phone calls. I became really concerned when Sam seemed to know exactly what was going on in every meeting we had. There was a leak in their office. I told them about the calls; they listened and then seemed to ignore me. I thought, "I can't understand this. Someone is giving Sam information." When I met with them to discuss the case, I stared at each one, wondering who was passing details of our conversation to Sam. The situation was very stressful. I didn't know whom to trust.

In an attempt to alleviate my fears, Ben tried to reassure me everything would be all right. My heart wanted to believe him, but my head told me that their lack of concern and the leak should give me reason for concern. I felt so vulnerable.

The pressure we were under was intolerable. The court date had been postponed several times and a new date had not been scheduled.

One evening, Ben said, "It's your birthday. Let's get out of here and have dinner some place."

J.C., our new bartender, was more than capable of overseeing the pub. The guard from the front of the bar offered to accompany us, but the officer who was stationed at the rear of the building decided to come instead. His dress was impeccable and classy and the expensive clothes and jewelry he wore screamed money. He indicated that he knew Sam very well and did not like this assignment. As he escorted us into the restaurant, he kept his distance. Nothing was said, but we thought he must be on Sam's payroll.

It was difficult conducting business with guards everywhere. The customers were uneasy, but at the same time they liked to feel like they were part of something. They asked a lot of questions.

The guard who accompanied the children to school stayed there all day. After school, he brought them home. Mike Lynch, the guard assigned to Ben, traveled with him every day to his job. They got along well and had a lot in common. Both were working class men with families to care for.

"We need to be careful, and make sure we are not being followed." Mike cautioned.

Several weeks later, Mike began working with the bricklayers. He became bored and decided he might as well work and earn some extra money, rather than sit in his car all day. Their friendship lasted many years.

The guards were assigned to us twenty-four hours a day. Two guards worked the day shift and were then replaced by the two guards who would watch over us through the night. The same two men were assigned each day and night. The night guard at the rear of the building kept himself invisible. Sometimes they sat in unmarked cars; often they wandered around the premises. I tolerated them, but felt uncomfortable, wondering if they could be trusted. Did they really care about my family's safety, or was this just a job to them?

I kept Benny home these days instead of sending him to kindergarten. School was not that important right now. He was happy to comply and confessed that he did not like school, anyway. Besides, he was company for Marty who was now three. We celebrated Benny's fifth birthday on August 19, 1964. It was a quiet celebration. In the morning he liked to play pool with me and enjoyed singing his favorite songs on the jukebox. And with Halloween approaching, he was going to be Superman. He would stand on the table at the back of the pub shouting, "Watch me fly, Mommy." Then he would jump off the table, pleased with himself as I stood there to catch him. He was adorable in his costume and I cautioned him to be careful for fear he would trip and hurt himself.

Donna and Patricia were at the parochial school in one area; he was at a public school elsewhere. I didn't want the children separated. Besides, I knew he preferred to stay home with me.

CHAPTER 35: FRIDAY

It was another Friday, like so many Fridays, on October 23rd, 1964. It was cold. I bundled the children up for school and Ben went to work. Ben and Mike were now traveling together in Mike's car. Even though we no longer cashed checks, the bar remained busy on a Friday. Since Art was there to help me, we handled the Fridays with ease. I looked forward to Ben returning home from work that day, as I felt uneasy

There was something different about this particular Friday. Ben had wakened that morning irritable. Neither one of us had slept well. We snapped at each other over the slightest thing. The toast was overcooked. The tea was too hot. It was silly, but somehow we found fault in each other, which was not normal. The kids were getting ready for school and could sense the tension in the room.

I smiled at them. "Everything is fine, we are tired this morning." Changing the subject, "Did you girls sleep well?" They nodded their heads in a yes.

The weather was dreary and I felt unsettled. The events of the past few weeks were taking its toll on us. I felt jumpy all day as if I was expecting something to happen.

I thought, "I will be happy when Ben comes through that door and I know he is here."

Ben came home from work early that day. Prior to coming upstairs, he spoke to the guards and asked if they needed anything before they took up their positions. They shook their heads. The one guard walked towards the alley at the back of the building and stayed out of sight. The other officer who was stationed in the front of the tavern usually wandered around interacting with the customers.

Ben acknowledged his customers before going upstairs to change his clothes. Benny was on the porch standing on a chair leaning out the window. Ben scolded him. He pulled the chair away and slammed the window shut.

"You can't hang out the window like that, what if you fell?" He spoke rather harshly. Benny said he was sorry and pouted; Ben rubbed his head with affection. "You need to be careful, Son."

He returned downstairs and greeted his customers. He frequently had a few drinks with them so I could leave to prepare dinner. When J.C. arrived to take over the bar, they usually greeted each other and conversed for several minutes prior to returning upstairs to the apartment. The next four hours belonged to us for some much needed rest and time together.

Ben always went downstairs just before midnight to take over and close the bar in compliance with our 2 AM license. This was our routine every Friday.

I began getting the children ready for bed. Donna was making her first communion on Sunday and wanted to try the dress on again for the tenth time. Our younger daughter, Patricia, wanted a white dress too. I assured her that her turn would come.

The boys were roughhousing and I said, "Enough. Come on, boys, it's time for bed."

Benny liked to sing his favorite song standing on a chair and singing as loud as he could. "Dinah, won't you blow; Dinah, won't you blow your horn, horn, horn."

I smiled at them; they were having such fun. Marty tried to climb onto the chair with him, but I again said, "Enough," in as stern a voice as I could muster. They ran to their room, giggling.

I tucked them into their beds. Benny was on the top bunk. Martin was on the bottom bunk. Their bed was by the window just off the porch. The girls were on the other side of the room in their bunk bed. Donna wanted the top bunk. Trisha had the bottom bunk. They were happy.

I sat for a few minutes relaxing, drinking a cup of coffee and smoking a cigarette. Benny came back out of the bedroom for that extra hug. I put him on my knee; I squeezed him and kissed him. He nuzzled his head under my chin, and he said, "I love you, Mommy."

I replied, "I love you, too. Goodnight, my little champ." Content, he scurried back to his bed. I loved them so much.

CHAPTER 36: THE FIRE

On October 23rd, 1964, sometime prior to midnight, I was awakened by loud voices. At first I was unsure if the voices were coming from the television, which I often left on while falling asleep, or if someone was calling me. When I finally gathered myself, I looked at the clock; it was just before midnight. Ben usually was downstairs at the bar by this time, but had slept in. Fatigue had settled in from the busy week.

I reached over and nudged him, myself still half asleep, "Wake up, you have slept in." I said, "There is a commotion downstairs." He grunted as he stirred.

Suddenly without warning, a large rock sailed through the window, shattering the glass and landed on the bed. We both bolted up at the same time. The voices were growing louder. We soon realized they were coming from below our bedroom window.

"What the hell was that for?" Ben exclaimed. Sitting up in bed and looking at the rock, we knew something was wrong. It took us a moment to get our bearings.

I asked anxiously, "What is it? What is going on?"

"I don't know," he replied, rubbing his eyes. He jumped out of the bed first and stumbled over to the window. He peered out, still unclear as to what was happening.

"What is it?" he shouted, shoving the broken glass to the side, then pushing up the window. He put his head out the opening; there was an outcry from the people standing screaming below. The noise was deafening.

Ben recognized most as customers and shouted back to them, "What's going on?" They were standing outside the tavern door on the sidewalk looking up at him. He detected fear in their voices as the screams became louder and more frantic. Everyone was shouting at the same time so he could not grasp what they were saying.

I groped around in the dark, trying to find my clothes. My mind filled with dread at the thought that something terrible had happened. Ben needed to get downstairs.

I thought to myself, Friday nights are the worst. There was always some altercation or other problem with the customers. Ben shoved me behind him, still not sure what had occurred. The customers from the tavern had not moved from below the window.

Their cries were more urgent. "It's a fire, Ben. The building is on fire; you need to get out."

"Where is the fire?" I shouted to Ben as I stumbled to the door of the bedroom. Grey smoke was billowing on the back porch. It looked like a whirlwind of clouds. Moonlight shone through the haze.

"My God" I shouted in horror, "There is smoke on the porch. It looks like it's on fire."

The porch was next to the children's room. Terror gripped my heart. Ben stood behind me, trying to get his wits together. We could see the length of the house from our room. The apartment was small and the back porch was engulfed in grey smoke. The smell was drifting into the living room where we stood. You could feel and smell the heat.

The shouting continued from below, "We have called the fire department. Get out, come out the window, we will catch you. Get out."

Their voices were shrill and fear rose in my chest until I felt it was difficult to breathe. The grey smoke on the back porch was getting thicker and darker and the odor was sharp. We could hear the crackling of the fire. The lights were still on and the smoke looked like swirling clouds dancing in a haze. We stood in the living room at the door before entering the kitchen. The children were asleep in the bedroom just off the porch. Ben was already fully clad. He had just lain down on the bed to catch a few hours before going downstairs. He looked at me and I saw the terror in his eyes.

His voice was strained and raspy when he spoke. "Stay here, I will get the kids and hand them to you, take them to the window and hand them out. The boys will catch them, but I need to move fast. Don't worry, I will get them." He assured me.

First he headed to the larger window in the living room and threw it open. Then he ran down the hall through the kitchen to their room, disappearing in the clouds of black smoke, which now filled the area.

I stood at the door watching the smoke as it became darker and bottomless. A feeling of panic started to overcome me when I could no longer see him. He entered their room and quickly reached down for our youngest son, Marty, and carried him to me. I reached my arms out to grab my child, but he went past me. He did not stop for me to put the child out. I watched anxiously as he carried Marty to the window and dropped him to waiting arms.

The crowd screamed and shouted, "We have him." Marty woke from his sleep and not knowing what was going on, started to cry. He was only three years old. I could hear the crowd consoling him. Ben ran back quickly towards the children's bedroom.

He shouted, his voice stressed, "I am going to take them out one at a time. I don't want to frighten them. You stay here."

I did not answer, only nodded my head, unable to move. Fear gripped my heart and the same apprehension was evident on his face. My chest was so tight that my breathing became shallow as I gasped for air.

Suddenly, it was pitch black; the electricity had shorted out. The darkness was terrifying. A trickle of light fell through the front room window from a street lamp, but the back room off the porch was covered in obscurity. It was difficult to see the smoke now, but the smell was so strong it consumed the house. I was terrified; the stench was like burning wood. I felt, rather than saw Ben as he emerged from the bedroom with Patricia in his arms, assuring her all was okay.

"Mommy," she cried, trying to cling to me, but in one swoop Ben had her out the window. Once again, the men standing below caught her. She was safe. I said a silent prayer.

I started to go towards the kitchen to their bedroom when Ben pulled me back. I could feel the heat from the flames that were licking the wood on the porch.

"You need to get out of here," he shouted, "or we will all die."

"I can't, I can't leave," I cried," I can't leave the kids. I want to see that they are all right."

Ben shoved me aside. I began to panic as he crawled towards the bedroom knowing the fear he felt. He seemed to be gone a long time and suddenly he was crawling on the floor towards me.

"I can't get back in there. I can't breathe," he whispered. The smoke is so thick, I can't see."

"I'm not leaving without the kids. I can't." I whispered.

"You have to get out now," he grabbed me and held me tight. "You need to get out. I'll come out, too, and see if I can get up the stairs."

"No, no!" I screamed. "I'm not going. I can't go."

"We need to get out or we will both die!" he cried out and pulled me towards the window.

"Please, please, the children will be scared. Please," I begged. Without another word, he lifted me out the window and dropped me into the waiting arms of the people below.

I fell hard and knew I had broken someone's arm as we both fell to the ground, but no one complained.

"Come down, Ben," they shouted, "the fire is getting worse." J.C. came running out of the tavern.

"Where is Ben?" he cried out and noticed I only had two of the children.

"He is still up there trying to get the other kids," I cried. "Please help him."

J.C. reached out and touched my shoulder. He ran back into the tavern and up the stairs where he was engulfed with thick, black smoke and flames. The fire was devouring the wood like a hungry vulture. He disappeared into the burning inferno and did not have a chance. J.C. would die at the foot of Benny's bed from smoke inhalation.

A few seconds later, Ben swung onto the sign and dropped to the ground then disappeared into the tavern towards the back stairs. He hoped that he would be able to reach the children that way. He did not realize that J.C. had already gone up the stairs and had not returned.

Someone put a coat around my shoulders. I nodded my head in acknowledgement and murmured thanks. It was October and cold and I did not have many clothes on. I shivered in anticipation and anxiety. The tears ran slowly down my cheeks as I prayed for the safety of my wonderful and lovely children who were my life.

"Oh my God," I prayed. "Please keep them safe, and please watch over them." I held my two children close to me, trying to comfort them and assuring them everything would be fine even though I felt in my heart that it would not. Terror strangled my throat as Ben rushed back out of the tavern, his face sunken. I could see the tears in his eyes as he came by my side.

"I can't reach them," he whispered. "J .C. has gone up the stairs and has not returned and the stairs are on fire. The smoke is so thick I can't see."

"Please, Ben," I cried in a hoarse voice. "We must get up there somehow. Please." Mrs. Comedecca, the lady from next door, came and took the two children.

Hope rose in my heart when I heard the sirens and saw the fire department arrive. Everyone was shouting at the same time.

"Up there, up there, up there; there are kids up there."

"How many children are there?" they shouted.

"There are two, two in the back bedroom; you need to hurry."

They threw a ladder against the wall to climb up to the window. Suddenly I looked up and saw Donna standing at the open window.

I cried out, "Oh my God."

"Mommy, Mommy," her voice filled with fear. I could see her beautiful face and held my breath knowing she was safe. Surely if she could come through the fire, our Benny would be safe, too. I prayed to God to answer my prayers and save my son.

The fireman climbed the ladder quickly and handed her to another fireman. Ben picked her up in his arms and handed her to me. She was crying softly. There was not a mark on her.

"I was scared," she cried and said, "I could not find you, and I was scared." I held her close.

Ben took her next door to the neighbor. She saw her brother and sister. Keeping in the role of the big sister, she went to them and they clung together. She was shivering from the cold and sobbing. Neighbors came and put blankets around them.

She turned to her father and said, "Where is Benny? I don't see Benny?" He could not answer her.

He finally said, "We will all be fine, I know we will all be fine."

I had said this through my own tears, "We will all be fine." It was almost like a prayer; God, how I wanted to believe this. Ben tried to reassure them. I tried to reassure myself.

Mrs. Comedecca was our next-door neighbor. She was a nice lady. She had invited the children into her house. She looked at him as he brought Donna to be with her siblings. There was sorrow in her eyes.

"Leave them here," she said softly, "I'll take care of them." Even though they had lived next door for many years, we had only said a "hello" now and then when we saw each other. They never came into the bar. The children knew them, but we did not.

I heard Ben shouting, "What do you mean the fire hydrant does not work?"

The fireman said, "There is no water in this hydrant. We need to try one up the street." They looked at each other, and then the customers and the firemen raced up the street, dragging the hose a whole block to find a fire hydrant that worked.

Another fireman climbed the ladder and went through the window to try and rescue our son. I watched as he entered and a few moments later reemerged. He came down the ladder empty handed.

He looked at us and said in a soft voice, "We did not bring the right equipment to go into the fire, I am sorry. It is out of hand. We did not realize the fire was this bad and we do not have any masks to enter."

The fire department took too long in coming, even though they had been called several times by anxious customers and neighbors. Although they were only a few blocks away, we calculated it took them at least thirty minutes. Once they came, they were ill prepared, not possessing the right equipment, and the fire hydrant, which was just outside the tavern door, had no water.

"This can't be happening," I cried out. My heart sank as Ben and I stood together. The tears were streaming down our faces quietly as hope began to fade.

He decided to run back into the tavern, hoping he could get up the stairs somehow. The fire department finally came down the alley with their hoses and water.

They were gone too long. Everyone wanted to help. They dragged the hose into the tavern to the stairwell where the fire was burning. The water gushed onto the red-hot flames. You could hear the sizzling of the scorching fire as the flames were put out, the smoke billowing into the sky.

After that, they were able to enter the building. Time was of the essence, but this had taken too long. I had not seen Ben for some time. I stood motionless as the tears ran down my face. I knew what I had to face and wondered if I had the courage to do so.

I continued to pray, "Don't let it be so. Please, God." Ben returned, his head was bent low, his shoulders dropped. He was crying. He took my hand, looked at me, pulled me towards him and held me. The tears streaming silently down our faces.

"He is gone," he said, "he is gone." He was only five years old. A part of me died that night. Around us, the customers and our neighbors were crying.

It was a sad night; tragedy affects a lot of people.

SUNDAY, OCTOBER 13, 1963

CHICAGO'S AMERICAN

Hunt Arson in Fire Fatal to

Authorities are investigating the possibility of arson in a fire which claimed the lives of 5-year-old Bernard McCluskie, son of a witness against hoodlum Sam De Stefano, and the boy's would-be rescuer.

The other fatality was James C. Pugh, 26, of 4054 W. Carroll av., a bartender in Ben's Place, a tavern at 718 N. Albany av. owned by the McCluskies, who live in a 5-room apartment above it.

Thomas F. Braun, 26, of 710 N. Albany, told police he saw three men drive up to the rear of the building late Friday night and that one man got out and threw an object to the second floor porch.

Saw Porch Burst into Flame

Sparks, as if from a lighted fuse, came from the object, according to the witness, and the porch burst into flame.

Investigators, however, were unable to find any evidence of such a fire bomb, but the probe is continuing.

Benjamin McCluskie, 34; his

wife, Norma, 31, and their four children were awakened as flames swept to their apartment. McCluskie lowered Patricia Lynn, 7; Martin, 3, and his wife from a front room window to the outstretched arms of a policeman and tavern patrons.

Leap Thru Flames

The father tried to reenter the bedroom to save the other children but was forced to leap to the ground. Another daughter, Donna Marie, 3, broke thru flames to a front window and was carried down a ladder by firemen. Bernard was trapped in the bedroom.

Pugh, meanwhile, leaped thru a wall of flames to dash up the burning rear stairway, but apparently died of smoke inhalation before reaching the boy.

The surviving children were treated for smoke inhalation at the Walther Memorial hospital.

Under Police Guard

Because the state was considering calling Mrs. McClus-

kie as a witness in the pending trial of De Stefano on a charge of conspiracy to commit perjury, the building had been under around-the-clock police guard for the last 6 weeks.

Lt. Robert J. Lynskey, a task force commander, said that originally both the front and rear of the building had been guarded, but that the rear guard was withdrawn several weeks ago in the belief it was not needed.

Robbed in 1962

Policeman James A. Daniels was on duty in front of the tavern at the time of the fire and helped rescue one child.

In October, 1962, three men robbed Ben's Place of $1,500, but Mrs. McCluskie shot one bandit in the shoulder as he fled.

The alleged robbers, including a wounded man, later were arrested and brought to trial, but were acquitted when several witnesses, including Mrs.

McCluskie, were reluctant to testify and failed to identify any of the suspects.

State's attorneys investigators later accused De Stefano of paying a $1,000 bribe thru Charles Grimaldi, a bartender, to two women to insure their silence and also of intimidating witnesses.

CHAPTER 37: ARSON?

Ben and the children were taken to Walter Memorial Hospital and treated for smoke inhalation. He went next door to get the children.

He sobbed as he told them, "Our Benny is gone." The children could not stop crying. He took Marty in his arms and pulled the girls close to him.

Gently he said, "Come along, we need to leave now." He thanked the lady who also was crying. The fire had been broadcast on television. Many friends came to the tavern to assist us in any way they could.

In the small hours of the morning, Ben's brother Frank and his wife Marie came and took the children home with them. Marie put them in the bathtub as they were covered with black soot. She was trying to distract their attention from what had happened. The children were inconsolable; no amount of soothing was going to help.

She tucked them in bed and gently explained to them that we would soon come." She added, "Everything is going to be okay." Exhausted, the children eventually fell asleep.

Ben left to identify Benny's body. He said, "I'll go and identify him. You can go to Marie and Frank's house or you can wait for me."

I whispered, "I'll wait here. I just can't go and see him like that, I just can't,"

He replied through his tears. "I understand. It's okay. I'll go."

I waited inside the tavern door, watching the police and firemen doing their job. When he returned, he was a broken man. His face stained with tears. I was ashamed that I did not have the courage to identify my own son.

When Ben returned, we went to Frank's house. It was morning and we were tired. Marie gave me a sleeping pill.

"You need to sleep, now," she said softly. The children were already gone. I was glad. I felt I could not face them and was not ready to explain what had happened.

I called my mother. The phone hardly rang when she answered.

I was sobbing and she asked, her voice a whisper, "Which one is it?" She said, "I have been up all night. I had a premonition."

The next day, my mother flew to Chicago to be by my side. Ret and Packy came and took the children to their home. They felt our sorrow. When my mother arrived, Packy returned and brought her to his home so she could be with our children.

"It will only be for a few days," I explained to her. I felt her strong arms around me as she held me tight.

Robert, 19. The couple also a boy friend will drowned
have an adult daughter other w

SAT OCT 24/64

Blaze Kills Hero, Child
in Guarded Building

[Continued from page 1]

condition that they not identify three men charged with robbing the McCluskie tavern in 1962.

Both women testified at the robbers' trial, but did not identify any of them.

Leahy questioned a neighbor of the McCluskies who said he saw 3 men drive up to the rear of the building and throw what appeared to be a sparkler thru the porch window.

The neighbor, Thomas F. Braun, 26, of 710 N. Albany av., said he saw the men from his second floor apartment 2 houses away.

Listed as Undetermined

Investigators were unable to find any evidence of a sparkler or anything which could have started the fire.

The police bomb and arson squad listed the cause of the blaze as undetermined.

Damage was estimated at $4,500 by Chief Albert Prendergast, 2d division fire marshal.

De Stefano is to face the charge of conspiring to commit perjury with Charles Grimaldi, a bartender, whom police say was the middle man.

The bribe was allegedly paid to alter testimony in the robbery trial of Frank Santucci, 38.

Several days after Santucci was wounded in a holdup of the McCluskie tavern in 1962, he was arrested in a Stone Park apartment.

He was positively identified by four witnesses in the tavern as one of the holdup men. Mrs. McCluskie had shot one of the robbers, identified as Santucci, in the shoulder as he fled.

When Santucci came to trial, the witnesses, including Mrs. McCluskie, were reluctant to testify and Santucci went free.

Witnesses are Frightened

State's attorney's police learned that witnesses had been terrorized.

De Stefano, a convicted bank robber and rapist, is scheduled to go to trial Monday on a charge of fraudulent voting. He is charged with voting without having had his rights restored after he was released from prison.

Arrested with Santucci for the McCluskie robbery were Anthony Donato, 51, and Robert Chessher, 34. They, too, were acquitted.

Santucci, having avoided jail for years, pleaded guilty on July 17, 1963, to burglary and was sentenced to 2 to 4 years.

Fire Kills Young Son Of Bribe-Case Witness

Continued from Page 1

derson, 25, of 1428 N. Fairfield, and Lorton Watkins, 39, of 542 N. Sawyer.

They were taken to Walther Memorial Hospital with the three surviving children. All five were given emergency treatment.

DeStefano is accused of trying to bribe Mrs. McCluskie and Mrs. Rita Burns, 27, a kitchen helper, to commit perjury by not identifying gunmen who held up the tavern in October, 1962.

The state's attorney's office has alleged that DeStefano and a former bartender at the tav-

ern, Charles Grimaldi, arranged the bribe.

Mrs. McCluskie fired five shots at two men who invaded the tavern, and thought she wounded one of them.

Three men were arrested in the robbery: Frank J. Santucci, who had a bullet wound in the shoulder; Anthony Donato and Robert Chesser.

Medical Research

WASHINGTON (AP)—The government, pharmaceutical industry and major voluntary health organizations are spending $1.5 billion this year on medical research, a report from the National Health Education Committee showed.

139

BOY, 5, AND MAN DIE

Fire Kills 2; Link To DeStefano Case

the young son of a woman who is to testify against a crime syndicate figure, and a bricklayer from her husband's squad died shortly before midnight Friday in a fire at the family apartment, 718 N. Albany.

A neighbor later told police he had seen three men drive up behind the apartment building housing the tavern and apartment and had seen one man hurl an object "showering

sparks" onto the apartment porch.

Albert Prendergast, 2nd division fire marshal, said the fire began on the rear porch.

Three other children of Mr. and Mrs. Bernard McCluskie were dropped to safety from the second-story window by the father before smoke and flames chased him from the apartment.

It was Bigaouette the proprietor, James C. Pugh, 26, of 4653 W. Carroll,

rushed into the flat in search of Bernard McCluskie Jr., 5.

Firemen found Pugh, a construction worker, dead on the floor." The boy's body was found in bed.

Police have maintained a 24-hour guard at the McCluskie tavern since Mrs. Norma McCluskie, 30, was named as a witness against syndicate loan shark Sam DeStefano in a perjury case.

Patrolman James Danieds, who was stationed in front of

the building, said he noticed nothing unusual Friday night.

However, Thomas F. Braun, 26, a dock worker who lives at 718 N. Albany, said he had seen the car containing three men behind the McCluskie place shortly before the fire.

Police and fire department arson squads were investigating.

Police Lt. Thomas Hayes gave this account of the fire: McCluskie, napping in the apartment, was awakened, he

smoke. He managed to rouse three of his children, Don, Marie, & Patricia Lynn, and Martin.

McCluskie dropped the youngsters to several patrons of the tavern, who had gathered beneath a window. He was driven out of by apartment by smoke before could reach Bernard Jr.

Two tavern patrons were killed by flying glass, They were identified as Judith, he

Turn to p.

CHAPTER 38: MY MOTHER

This is a moment when I can reflect on my wonderful parents and family. They loved me and felt my sorrow as their own. Mama was a strong, caring woman who enjoyed taking care of everyone.

I recalled those wonderful days when she would rise in the morning, always cheerful. It was always important to her that we would start our day with a good breakfast. She put the coffee on for Papa. He liked his coffee black and strong and would add some of his homemade grappa, which was like moonshine. He would crack the shells of two raw eggs and tilt his head back as he drank its contents. I would shudder and could not imagine swallowing two raw eggs. That was his breakfast. Mama made pancakes, bacon, and eggs with toast for my two brothers, my sister and me. I loved her toast, as she had made the bread herself. The toast would be dripping with butter and homemade jam. My mouth would water just thinking about it.

My mother was a woman of great stature; a small lady with a big heart. Not quite five-feet tall, her jet-black hair was pulled into a bun and tied neatly behind her head. Her dark-brown eyes sometimes appeared sad. She emigrated from a small town in Italy called San Stefano Del Solo. A courageous woman, she traveled across Canada by train to join her sister when she was only seventeen.

After the fire, we rented an unfurnished apartment so our kids and my mother could be with us. The tavern was closed and the fire was under investigation.

Ben said, "We need to purchase some furniture so we can move in. Our kids need to be with us." They needed us and we needed them. I wanted to hold them close to my heart.

The apartment we rented was quite large. It was located on Keating Avenue, several streets further north of Chicago Avenue. A duplex, the owners lived on the first floor and our apartment was on the second floor. Our savings dwindled as we replaced furniture and clothing. We still had an obligation to pay for the liquor that had been delivered the day of the fire. The company offered us more time. Starting over again was not going to be easy.

The headlines screamed, ARSON, and the newspapers had a field day linking us up with Sam. The story was on the front page of every newspaper and on television. The media were outside the tavern daily, snapping pictures of the building and us. The reporters asked questions we could not answer. We were trying to get to grips with reality.

We told the reporters several times, "Please leave us alone."

(CHICAGO'S AMERICAN Photo by Cliff Oliver)

TRAGEDY SHOWING in her face, Mrs. Norma McCluskie hugs son Martin, 3, who saved from fire by heroic bartender before he died i further rescue efforts. Another Bernard Jr., 5, also was killed. At left is an aunt, Mrs. Marion McCluskie.

FATHER OF BOY who died, Bernard McCluskie Sr., carries another of his children from Fillmore police station. At right is Capt. Thomas Hayes. McCluskie is part owner of tavern whose bartender resued two McCluskie children.

Fire Kills 2; Gang Link Investigated

Building at 718 N. Albany in which two persons lost their lives and three suffered from smoke inhalation in a fire last night. Police are investigating possibility of arson.

J,C, PUGH

Some accounts in the newspaper were accurate, while others were not. One story that always upset me was about the second guard. Lt. Robert Lynskey was a task-force commander who said he withdrew the guard from the rear of the building several weeks before as he felt the guard was not needed. This was not true as both guards were there the night of the fire. That night, the guard at the rear of the building just disappeared. One paper said that I was not home. This was also false. I was always home. Another reported that the firemen could not get up the stairs because they were blocked. The stairs to the bedroom where the children slept was clear. J.C.'s ability to get to the bedroom was proof that there was a clear path to the bedroom and the children.

In the days that followed, we had a viewing for our son and J.C. at the same location, Hallowell Funeral Home, which was located at 2938 North Lincoln Avenue. I stood at the casket for a long time, holding his small hands wrapped around a crucifix. I opened his tiny fists and took it from him, holding it close to my heart. Only his little face was visible, most of his body was covered with a sheet. He did not look the same and suddenly I realized he must have been badly burnt. I found this unbearable. I wanted everyone to remember him as that sweet little boy who warmed my heart. I bent down and stroke his head, kissed him and touched his hands one last time, whispering goodbye. He was cold; my tears would not stop. Suddenly, I reached up and closed the casket.

I was sad when J.C.'s wife, brought her two children to the viewing. The children were too young and did not understand. They were crying when they saw their father lying in his casket. J.C.'s mother, brother and sisters also came from Tennessee to attend the funeral. They were very kind. I knew their hearts were also broken.

We had an insurance policy for our son and the proceeds covered both funerals. The cost of the funeral in 1964 for each of our loved ones was approximately $846.

The two coffins were in the same room and hundreds of people came to the viewing. Some who came were strangers. Others were customers and many were friends. Sam and his men also came, causing a commotion at the door. At first, the guards stopped them from entering. They then decided to allow them in with a warning because the altercation was causing a disruption. I did not look up and wondered if Chuck came or if he felt any shame or remorse. He knew all the children, but then he was a man who had children of his own and did not acknowledge them. Ben said Chuck did come, but stood silently in the background at the back of the funeral parlor where he would not be noticed.

Sam stood in front of me where I sat with my mother. I did not look up, but could sense his presence. This was not an appropriate time to feel angry. He tried to push an envelope into my hand, which I rejected. How dare he come here and show such disrespect? I could not look at him; there was such hate in my heart. He handed the envelope to my mother. She took it and thanked him, not knowing who he was. He spoke to her softly in Italian and she nodded her head. I did not hear what he said. He walked away.

Sam went and sat next to Chuck after he was sure everyone was aware of his presence. They only stayed for a few minutes, when a guard came over and escorted them out.

Sam shouted so everyone could hear him, "I had nothing to do with this." The guard accompanied him out the door with a friendly push. Sam had made his point.

Mass was held at Saint Mathews Church prior to the departure to the cemetery. His white casket sat near the altar. Due to the crowd, many people had to stand at the back of the parish. The ceremony was wonderful, and the beautiful music filled my heart. The angels were above the altar and I prayed to them to keep him safe.

Our Benny was laid to rest at St. Joseph's Cemetery. We stood by his gravesite. Ben was holding my arm, and mama stood beside me, both of us sobbing uncontrollably. Ben choked back his tears.

"I don't want him in the ground," I whispered. "Please don't let them put him in the ground."

Ben motioned to the pallbearers. The men sat the casket down beside the site as the priest said prayers.

Ben pulled me, "Come on, we are going home."

I cried, "I don't want to go home. I want to stay here for a while.

"Norma, you can't, come on," he gently led me to the car.

I could not bear the thought that my child would be put into the ground. I wanted to tear up the earth and take him in my arms, hold him once more. That was not possible; I knew he was gone.

CHAPTER 39: OUR HOME

Several weeks passed before we went back to the tavern. We decided it was the proper time to see if we would be allowed inside the building. Some neighbors were standing on the sidewalk, sadness etched on their faces. We were apprehensive about getting out of our car. As we stood silently by the tavern door we looked up at the burnt building. The windows were open and the curtains were blowing in the breeze. The building looked weary and sad.

We were experiencing sadness now, but I needed to remember happier times, this was our home. I thought back to our beginning, how excited we had been. The purchase of the tavern was a new beginning. Ret had decided the apartment was too small for them, so they found an apartment on Ohio Street just blocks away.

Coming from the kitchen below, the first flight of stairs came to a broad landing before turning the corner to the flight of stairs leading to the apartment. The boxes of liquor were stored on the landing next to a small refrigerator, but because of the breadth of the landing, it was easy to pass and climb the stairs to the porch above. The door off the porch opened into a large kitchen. To the left, next to the kitchen, was a bedroom also facing the porch; this was where the children slept. The bathroom was next to the kitchen, adjacent from the side door leading to the street, the door we seldom used. Our thoughts were that the kids would forget to lock it, and anyone could come into the house.

Behind the bathroom were the living room and another bedroom, both rooms facing Albany Avenue. The apartment was adequate for us. The kitchen was large enough for a washer and dryer and any appliance we wished to put in it. I loved big kitchens. We were excited about our new home.

The arrangement worked out well. The four of us had discussed how we would split the hours; pay the mortgage and rent, the utility bills, phone bills and any other bills associated with the business. Each one of us would have some spending money. We also discussed how we would take care of the children. Ret walked three of her children to school every day before coming to the tavern with her youngest daughter. Ben closed most nights; therefore he generally came downstairs later in the morning. Usually, I picked up all the school-aged children after school. Upon my return, Ret took her children home. Everything seemed to be falling into place.

CHAPTER 40: MISTAKES

The fire chief, Albert Prendergast, was standing at the door of the pub. He was the second division fire marshal and was on duty on the night of the fire. Albert claimed the fire had started on the back porch. When he saw us, he offered his condolences. We asked why? Why had they come with no fire equipment? Why was there no water in the fire hydrant? Why did it take so long for the fire department to arrive?

I could see the pain on his face. He replied, "I'm sorry. We all make mistakes." These mistakes cost two lives. His apology offered little consolation.

He said, "The fire is still under investigation, it will be a few weeks before you can enter the building."

The days that followed were a blank. I walked around in a catatonic state and could not sleep. Ben was not much better. Both of us cried a lot. We couldn't come to terms with our loss. Frank and Marie were kind and took care of us as if we were children.

I went to the cemetery at every opportunity and spent quiet moments with my son. I knew once we were back in the tavern this would not be possible. I missed him so much and was tortured by the fact he was beyond my reach. Ben said his soul was in heaven, but it did not ease the pain. Death was so final.

Several weeks later, the authorities allowed us to enter the building. It was a heart-wrenching scene. We stood at the entrance of the pub, trying to adjust our thoughts. The first recollection I had was the strong smell of liquor, which filled my nostrils. Next, I could smell a musky odor throughout the bar that filled the room. The air was stale and reeked of old beer that was still sitting in the glasses half full.

My eyes glanced over to the counter and I saw sandwiches partially eaten, molding in their wrappers. The stench was pungent. There were bugs on the sandwiches. I shivered. The sour smell of bar rags that were used to clean the countertop and were lying in a heap on the floor, their odor lingered in the air. The false ceiling that hung over the entire bar area was hanging down in tatters. The bar was in disarray. Ben began to straighten out the bottles of liquor adjusting them on the shelves in the order he thought they should be. He walked around the bar, putting the stools in their proper place. I watched him as he picked up a newspaper off the floor. With the paper, he took a swat at the flies. I thought, *He just needs to keep his mind occupied.* He sat beside me at the bar and spoke out loud, his voice strained.

"The place smells terrible." I had not moved and was staring into space; not wanting to think or feel. He touched my hand and said gently, "It's going to be all right; we'll get through this. Okay?"

I looked up and tried in vain to smile. I was afraid to speak as I felt my voice would crack with emotion. I wanted to be brave. We sat at the bar for a long time, afraid to go upstairs. Eventually, we climbed the stairs. Ben went first and I followed. The smell of burnt wood was strong and familiar. The tears slipped down my cheeks.

I could only think of my child, "My poor darling. Dear Lord, why did my baby have to endure this?"

The smell of smoke was everywhere. It surprised us that the stairs were only charred. Ben said, "Careful you don't get a sliver from the banister," He reminded me about this as it had happened to him once. It seemed a long time ago. My memory recalled that day how he had to go to the hospital emergency room where he had the sliver of wood removed. It was buried deep under his nail and was painful.

We stood on the porch for some time, staring out the window. Our attention focused on the backyard, where some of our furniture lay. The firemen had tossed it out the window. To turn around and face the door to the kitchen was painful; knowing when we entered the apartment the horror would come back to us. The door to the apartment was closed. The window next to the door in the children's room was open. I felt my heart miss a beat, and was afraid to look at it. Benny had slept on the other side of that window. Now he was gone.

Ben squeezed my hand and held it tight. We entered the apartment slowly, afraid of what we would see. I wondered where they had found J.C.'s body. I hoped I was not standing on the spot, as somehow it seemed sacrilegious.

We stood silently in the kitchen before turning our attention to the children's bedroom. The cedar chest Mama had given to me stood against the wall. It was charred and I remembered all the beautiful contents that were inside that Mama wanted me to have. My eyes were focused on the chest; I wanted to divert my attention from his bed. My hands touched the chest and I opened it carefully. Everything was still intact, but smoke had managed to seep inside, destroying its contents. My heart was heavy.

At the same moment, we tentatively raised our eyes and looked at his bed. Our hands clasped tightly as the pain ripped through us both, passing from one to the other. The mattress was gone, the top of the bed charred. Choking back the tears, we could visualize him on that top bunk by the window. He never had a chance. The windowpanes were broken and the glass was still on the floor beside his bed. He slept through the fire and had not suffered.

It seemed like an eternity as we stood there, each in our own thoughts. Ben moved first and sat down on a chair in the kitchen.

I looked away and turned my attention to the rest of the

apartment, kicking the burnt ashes on the floor. Everything was destroyed, the wallpaper hung off the walls, and the linoleum on the floor was in tatters. Parts of the ceiling had caved in. The plaster had fallen on the top of the refrigerator and stove leaving them black and wet. Small pools of water had formed on the floor. Ben rose from his chair and started moving things around. He closed the refrigerator door, picked up chairs and put them in their proper place. I watched him in silence, consumed by the emptiness that filled every inch of me.

The smell of burning wood clung to every crevice of the room. The stench filled our nostrils and followed us as we moved into the living room and on to our bedroom. The damage was more from the water, but the dominating aroma of smoke was everywhere: in the sofa, the curtains and the carpet. I shivered, realizing my hair also smelled of smoke. I felt nauseated, wondering if the smell would ever go way.

I entered our bedroom, trying desperately to keep my mind occupied, and stared at our belongings in the closet. Several items I lifted and held close. The majority of our clothes had to be thrown away; there could be no reminders of that night. I could not get the smell of burning wood out of my head. I sat on our bed, sobbing loudly. Ben sat beside me holding my hand. We sat there for a long time.

Ben began coughing as if he was choking. "The smell of smoke is strong," he said. "I can hardly breathe. I can't stop thinking about that night..." and his voice trailed off into his own thoughts. He rose up and put his head out the window as if to breathe in some fresh air.

After a few moments he turned quickly towards me, "Let's go home, Norma, I feel sick, we can come back again."

I looked at him and thought, *This* is *our home*.

Anything of value was gone. Our jewelry and the money we had in the safe had disappeared. The large bottle of loose change the children were saving for Christmas and a movie camera we had just purchased to take pictures of the children had vanished. I thought we never had a chance to use the camera. I wanted to search for the camera and suddenly realized it was not significant. It was a small thought that was not important. However, these thoughts run through your head.

You wonder who would take these things, knowing we already lost so much. I wondered how we were going to be able to live here again. It was going to take a great deal of courage. Everywhere there were signs of our son. I could still visualize him standing on the table downstairs, dressed in his Superman costume, asking, "Why can't I fly?" I could hear him singing his favorite song, "Dinah, Dinah won't you blow your horn, Dinah won't you blow, blow, blow...."

There were many questions to which we had no answers. What had caused the fire? A delivery of liquor came that day; the cases were piled on the landing as always. Someone had removed them. I remember thinking, "We still have to pay for that liquor," then wondered who had taken them away. Was there something in the boxes that could set the fire off? The Syndicate owned most of the liquor companies. Could they be responsible? Or did someone come into the tavern and slip into the back and start the fire? No one was detained. I wondered to myself *That night, did anyone see any strangers in the bar? Who did the police question?* We knew nearly everyone. After all, it was a neighborhood pub. Did the authorities query anyone? Fires need to start somewhere. The fire department, the police and the State's Attorney's Office did not have any answers. We were told, "The boxes were taken away as evidence. Nothing could be salvaged."

Bernard McCluskie and his wife Norma stand with a few salvaged items as they view ruins of their tavern and upstairs apartment where their son died in fire. (Sun-Times Photo by Ralp Arvidson)

CHAPTER 41: THE HOLIDAYS

My mother stayed with us for almost two months, but had to get back to take care of my father who was disabled. She wanted to be home for Christmas. I could not think about Christmas. It was the furthest thing from my mind.

Mama said, "You need to put a tree up for the kids and make an effort to have Christmas for them. They need everything to feel normal again."

"I will try, Mama." I smiled at her, grateful for her understanding and the time she spent with us. I would miss her, but needed time to be alone.

Ben had been working for a company off and on for some time. The weather was a factor and the job was not steady. Because it was Thanksgiving, the company gave him a turkey.

The foreman said, "Thought you could use this, Ben, for your family, it's Thanksgiving."

Ben thanked him and brought the turkey home. "Come," he said, "We always celebrate Thanksgiving." I looked at him and did not feel like celebrating. It was hardly a month gone by since we lost him. "Come on, Norma, we can invite a few friends, it would be good for the kids."

Mama said, "It will be good for you to have some friends over. You need to bring some happiness in the house for the kids." Finally, I agreed and said it would be okay. Ben invited his brothers, Frank and Pat, and their wives. He also invited Joe and Anne Trainor.

The evening began well. Mama cooked the turkey and set a lovely table. Anne brought her two sons, so the kids had company. I had not realized that Ben's brothers' wives were not friends. It had not crossed my mind, but I remembered I had not seen them in company together. After a few drinks, Pat's wife began to insult Frank's wife Marie, bringing up things about her past, and Marie fired back at her. The argument became heated and Ben pulled Pat's wife off Marie as she began to attack her. With unknown strength, he opened the back door and threw her down the stairs.

He was angry and turned to Pat, "Why in hell can't you control your wife? Do you not think we have been through enough? I'll call you a cab, take her home." Ben shook his head in disgust, "She acted up at the meal after the funeral at the Venetian Lounge and now... when in hell does this stop? She has upset my wife twice in the last couple of weeks and I am sick of her and her antics. You need to start taking control of your responsibilities." Ben apologized to our other guests, but they understood. They knew how she behaved as they had experienced problems with her themselves at other parties.

Our poor landlady, God only knows what she must have thought. My thoughts were, "So much for a happy Thanksgiving." Mama was quiet, realizing what a terrible strain we were under. She did not quite understand what was going on.

CHAPTER 42: REALITY

We needed to return our lives to a normal environment for the sake of the kids. It was already difficult going to a new school and trying to make new friends. I went to the tavern frequently, trying to salvage some of our keepsakes. Marty would go next door to play with the kids. I combed through the rubble in the apartment looking for memories.

I picked up one of our Benny's shoes and his Superman costume. I found his little red jacket he wore on Easter Sunday. He loved that jacket. I was upset that day, as I could not find his red top hat that he loved so much. I cradled them in my arms close to my chest and cried over each item as if my heart would break.

"This is so unfair, why him, why?" I could not answer my own question. If not him, who, or which one of my children was to be chosen? I could not have made that choice, so the good Lord made it for me. There were no answers, only questions.

Construction workers were doing repairs in the tavern area. I wanted to go through my possessions before they came upstairs to begin work. My fear was they would discard my things before I had a chance to look at everything.

"Please lady, take your time. We won't go upstairs for a while yet." I thanked them.

The possessions we lost meant nothing except for the items that pertained to our Benny. I wanted to hold them dear. It was as if I could bring him back. God, how I loved him. I would sit for hours sobbing. This was the only place I could be alone. If I went to the cemetery, the guard followed. At home, I had to remain positive for the kids.

I put up a small tree for the kids. I also tried to shop for them, but my heart wasn't in it. Several weeks before Christmas, it had been snowing non-stop, piling over the curb and spilling onto the sidewalks. There was no sign of snowplows. I continually looked out of the window for a glimpse of Ben, who had not come home yet. He seemed distraught this morning going to work, but there was no way he could have worked today. I worried as I looked out of the window. In the distance, I saw him trying to keep his balance on the mounds of snow.

I opened the door at the top of the staircase. As he came towards the stairs, I noticed he had been drinking. His body swayed and suddenly he fell through the window at the bottom of the stairs.

"Oh my God," I muttered and said, "Are you okay?"

"Yes," he whispered. "My shoes are slippery from the snow. I lost my balance..." There were tears in his eyes. I was horrified and apologized to the landlady.

Ben was finding it tough to come to grips with our son's death. All of this turmoil had been too much. I realized I would have to be the strong one. I thought of my mother and reached inside my soul for the strength I needed to go on.

CHAPTER 43: MOVING ON

Several weeks later in the early hours of the morning, unable to sleep, I lay on the sofa. I had many sleepless nights and did not want to disturb anyone. We still had a guard even though I felt it was unnecessary, but the State's Attorney's Office insisted. His unmarked car was parked outside our residence. Each time I left the apartment, he followed me. I never acknowledged him.

This particular night there was a loud bang that I thought was a car backfiring. I was awake in a flash and ran to the window. The guard jumped out of his car and began chasing a man down the street. Realizing, he could not catch him, he returned to his car and looked around.

He glanced up, saw me standing at the window, waved and proceeded to the front door. He said, "I need to use the phone; everything is fine. I was dozing and someone tried to rob me. My gun went off."

I spent many additional nights on the sofa after that. I often wondered what the landlady thought. I am sure she read the newspapers.

Just before Christmas, Ben decided to visit friends at the Venetian Lounge. The lounge was located on Chicago Avenue and Laramie Street around the corner from Albany Avenue.

One of the owners, Bob Frawley, was trying to encourage Ben to come and work for them. Being near Christmas, the bar was busy and had acquired many of our customers.

He said, "Come on, Ben, it will keep your mind occupied, you know everyone. Harry and I would love to have you aboard."

Ben smiled, "Thanks, but I like to be home as much as I can." He paused for moment, and then continued, "Maybe working would be good for me." Ben was deep in thought contemplating the offer and he did not hear the commotion at the door.

Chuck suddenly burst into the bar and stood for a moment scanning the room.

Noticing Ben sitting at the bar, he approached him. "I need to talk to you," he said. He appeared to be out of breath, as if he had been running. "I am sorry for what has happened, but Sam has asked for a favor. I know this is a bad time for you, but you know we have to go to court soon. Sam wondered if you could sign this paper for him. He wants you to testify on his behalf."

He pulled a piece of paper out of his pocket and handed it to Ben. Ben stared at the paper and shook his head.

"No," he said, "I can't sign anything." He crumpled the paper and handed it back to him in disbelief. How could Chuck ask this after all that had happened?

Chuck stared at him and in a strained voice said, "You know, Ben, I am your friend. This is where we have to part ways. I have to walk away." Chuck looked at him for a few more seconds, then turned quickly, lowered his head and walked out the door.

Ben sat and stared at the door. Sam wanted Ben to testify for him against Ret and I. For Chuck to ask for such a favor showed he was still in Sam's pocket. We never saw him again.

Arson was never proven. We never knew how the fire started. Our belief was that Sam and Chuck had something to do with it, but we did not know how to prove it.

The authorities were not particularly helpful. They said it was ruled an accident. The fire department used the term "combustion."

THE J.C. PUGH MEMORIAL BENEFIT DANCE

Saturday, December 19. 1994

Logan Square Masonic Temple

Chicago, Illinois

Featuring:

Bobby Johnston, Baritone

Jackie Howards Orchestra

Smolleys Country and Western Band

Chicago Highlanders Pipe Band

Irish Ceilidh Band and Dancers

J.C. PUGH

J.C. PUGH came to Chicago from a small town called Covington in the state of Tennessee

On the 23rd of October 1964, "J.C." was tending bar In Ben's Place at 718 N. Albany Ave when a fire broke out, trapping 5 year old Benny McCluskie in an upper bedroom. J.C. –without regard to his own safety entered the building in an effort to save the child. He was unsuccessful and both he and the child lost their lives in the fire.

This evening's program is designed to gather funds to assist the widow and two small children of this heroic young man—and equally important—to acknowledge publicly all our deepest respect and admiration for a hero……

John O'Donnell, President

George Hudson, Vice President (Pub)

John Mullins, Treasurer

Mrs. J. MacKinnon, Secretary

CHAPTER 44: BENEFIT DANCE

Many friends and several Irish pubs from the south side of Chicago organized a benefit dance in our honor. Although it had started out as a benefit dance for our family, it was decided that the dance should be for J.C.'s two children. Ticket sales and advertising for the dance were overwhelming. The J.C. Memorial Dance was held on December 19, 1964, at Logan Square Masonic Temple. J.C., a true hero and without regard for his own safety, had run through the flames to try and save our son. We were forever grateful for his bravery. Both had died, but neither will ever be forgotten.

A committee was formed and they decided that the proceeds from the dance would be placed in trust for his children. The funds would be available when they turned twenty-one. Ben was adamant that I go to the function with him. I was not up to the task, but because of his persistence, I agreed to attend. In their efforts to collect as much money as possible, many people had worked tirelessly to make this dance a success.

When entering the hall, I was extremely nervous and not prepared to face all the people.

Ben said, "Norma, relax. You know most of them. They are friends." I nodded my head and did my best to be sociable. I did know most of them. They were kind, but when I saw Benny's name on the program, I burst into tears and was inconsolable. Ben took me home.

The event was too soon after his death. I had not come to terms with my grief. I was happy the dance was a success. We worried about J.C.'s children. We had each other and our children and knew we would survive.

J.C.'s wife did not seem pleased that the money did not go directly to her, but put into a trust fund for the children. She had received compensation from Midwest Fence. With the funds, we were told she purchased a convertible and had a new boyfriend within a month. She took the kids to the pubs in the area, allowing them to run around unsupervised. Finally, some of the owners were compelled to tell her it was shameful. Giving the money to her was not the responsible thing to do.

CHAPTER 45: CONVICTIONS

I can't remember when the first court date was scheduled, probably in September of 1964. Because of the fire that occurred in October, it had been rescheduled several times. It was now scheduled for January 1965. I was not called to testify and can't remember much about it. It remains a blur in my mind. However, we were told to be present. At the courthouse, we entered a crowded elevator that took us to the courtroom where Sam was being held. A jury found him guilty. He took the verdict calmly and did not throw one of the tantrums he was noted for. We did not see Chuck that day, but assumed he would be tried separately.

Ret testified she had lied before the Grand Jury because she was afraid and felt threatened. She mentioned that her conscience bothered her, but was more fearful of Sam. Without her testimony, Sam would walk. She was the key to his conviction.

Sam had been in the county jail since December 6, 1964 for a one-year sentence for contempt of court, plus one to three years for illegally offering to vote. Now that he had been found guilty of conspiracy to commit perjury and tampering with a witness, he faced the possibility of five additional years. Judge Leighton filed a motion for a new trial by his attorney for Jan 22, 1965. Ultimately, he would appeal the jury charges and soon was free on bond.

To add insult to injury, several weeks after the trial I received a check from the State's Attorney's Office. The check was for a $125. The letter that came with the check thanked me for my service.

Why Chuck was not convicted at the same time as Sam was something I did not understand. Surely he was not going to walk away blameless. I wondered if he had a separate court date. For reasons that are unknown to me, he was never tried in court. I read or was told by someone that he claimed we had not pressed charges because we considered him a friend. That was not true. We never spoke to anyone about him. Chuck would have realized by now he was not a friend. Friends are people who trust each other. I never trusted him.

Every day I thought about the fire and our child. I finally came to the conclusion that we were an easy mark. My belief was that the fire was set to send a message to our ex-partners and us. It would have been harder to reach them in the suburbs. The tavern was an open target because we lived in a public place with easy access.

In all probability, the officer who was assigned to guard the back of the tavern was told to disappear. After all, this was Chicago and it was noted for its crooked police force and politicians. Whether he was bribed or threatened, I do not know. Would he have been on Sam's payroll? I can't even remember his name. I am certain Sam would have stopped at nothing to avoid prison. He was a man who hated to lose.

The decision would be made to set our place on fire to teach us a lesson. This task, however, would be delegated to Chuck. He knew our place well. The porch was old with dry wood and the fire would spread quickly. Unknown to them, the liquor that had just been delivered that day was stored on the landing and this would fuel the fire. He probably thought our customers would alert us. The timing of the fire always stuck in my mind: Friday at midnight. Chuck would know this was the time when Ben always came downstairs to take over and close the pub. He had worked for us long enough to know our routine.

JAN 13, 1965

CHICAGO TRIBUNE, WED

tefano Guilty in Perjury Case

De Stefano

o, 55, a crime
ark, was con-
.last Friday
ty jail cell,
xtensive dam-
risoner since
he year sen-
of court and

a one to three year sentence for
illegally offering to vote. De
Stefano faces another possible
sentence of one to five years on
the perjury conspiracy charge.

His wife, Anita, who sat
among spectators with their
three children, broke into tears
when the clerk in Judge George
C. Leighton's court read the
verdict. The jury deliberated
for an hour and 45 minutes.

The case against DeStefano
resulted from information de-
veloped from an informant in
the crime syndicate by Sgt.
James Kennedy of the Chicago
police Intelligence unit. Kennedy held a series of meetings
with the informant, then turned
the information over to the
state's attorney's office.

DeStefano was accused of
giving back $1,000 in robbery
loot to a woman tavern oper-
ator to change her testimony
in the trial of three men accused of robbing the tavern on
Oct. 5, 1962.

Mrs. Henrietta Burns, 29,
part owner of the tavern at
718 N. Albany av., had testified before the grand jury

identifying Robert Chessler,
36, as the man who burst
around the tavern and ap-
parently was the fingerman
for two armed robbers.

But when Chessler went on
trial with Frank Santucci, 36,
and Anthony DiDonato, 51,
Mrs. Burns testified that she
could not positively identify
any of them as having been
in the tavern.

She admitted on the witness
stand last week that she lied
in the robbery trial.

Mrs. Burns testified that several weeks after she identified Chessler before the grand
jury, DeStefano visited the tavern and offered her and her
partner, Mrs. Norma McCluskie, 31, $1,000 if no one identi-
fied Chessler during the trial.

When the robbery case was
tried all three men were
acquitted.

Judge Leighton set Jan. 27
for the filing of a motion for a
new trial by Julius Lucius
Echeles, attorney for De-
Stefano; and Jan. 28 for a
hearing on the new trial motion.

The fire was started by someone. If it were intended to dispose of us, it would have been set after hours. Killing us was not the purpose of the fire, I am certain that it was to scare us. Chuck would not do this himself. He could not come into the bar because he was well known by the customers. I am positive he helped Sam plan his dirty deed. In all probability he hired the person who set the fire and gave him the orders of how to execute it. Their intention was not to take lives, only to inform us they were in control.

Sam was furious because he had not persuaded me to change my testimony. Little did he know it would not be me that would seal his fate? He was used to being in command and having power over his situations. People feared him and always did his bidding. Two people died and I am sure Chuck had second thoughts. Their plan had backfired. In my mind everything had come full circle.

Sam must have been livid when he was indicted and Crimaldi was not. Somehow the charges had been dropped against Chuck. The State's Attorney's Office and the Feds were happy to get Sam; he had been on their list for a long time. They had other plans for Chuck; they planned to use him as a witness against Sam.

Charles Siragusa who was head of the Illinois Crime Investigating Commission believed Sam and Chuck had started the fire. Unfortunately, there was insufficient evidence to support this. According to the authorities, this line of inquiry was not pursued and was ruled inconclusive. The Feds were relying on Chuck to assist them by becoming a state's witness against Sam and he was given a reprieve. Their priority was to get Sam. They wanted to seriously hamper the loan shark business and to infiltrate the drug traffic.

CHAPTER 46: RETURN TO ALBANY AVENUE

In May 1965, we reopened the tavern. Max, our liquor salesman, arranged for a new shipment of liquor. Bill Glass, an attorney whom Max had introduced to us when we first purchased the pub, took care of the liquor license. Bill was essentially a nice guy and a prominent lawyer who had a large office on LaSalle Street in downtown Chicago. I can't remember what floor it was on in one of those high rises that oozed luxury. Bill was not a particularly attractive man. He was grossly overweight and displayed his large, protruding stomach with pride. He was overtly confident, cocky even, and fancied himself with the ladies.

Bill was always trying to impress, either giving you trinkets when you visited his office or a photo of himself from some branch of the service. I never could remember which service. In many ways, he was a good attorney. He had no problem in renewing your license or taking care of small incidents that cropped up in the bar business. He once helped Ben with a traffic violation, making it disappear. When Sam became involved in our lives, he backed away and was at a loss for words. He claimed this was not his area of expertise.

It became increasingly difficult paying a mortgage on the tavern and rent for an apartment. We had a commitment and knew we had to try and sell the business before we could move on. In the meantime, we moved back to Albany.

The things that had once seemed important were insignificant now. Benny's life was so much more important than anything we had ever strived for. Working hard and trying to save seemed pointless.

I realized we had been ill equipped to make decisions or understand the environment in the big city. The rules were so different here. I had been raised to respect the law. In Chicago, the law didn't command nor deserve respect. I had felt so safe at home, but Chicago was very different to the places where we grew up.

We dreaded the return to Albany Avenue, knowing we had to face our fears. It was a difficult time for the children and us. It was tough, not knowing how they felt. I had tried talking to them to explain what happened and why. They would stare at me, not saying a word, then hug me and cry softly. I told them everything would be all right as I fought back the tears. As soon as we opened the door of the tavern, the children rushed upstairs to see their new house. They were home. Before this, I had only brought Marty here with me, never the girls. Marty was a baby, he did not understand.

Ben and I sat quietly at the bar, trying to adjust ourselves for what we had to face. It was a beautiful day. It still was cold, but brisk, and the sun shone through the window, a ray of light and hope.

The pub smelled fresh of disinfectant and bleach, they were clean odors. There was a new ceiling, tiled in a light-grey color, and the walls were white. It looked nice. The floor had been replaced, a nice dark color with a pattern. I had cleaned the bar and the house on my many visits and the results were amazing.

The glasses glistened on the shelves. The place sparkled and the bar shone. The stools had been replaced. The liquor bottles were arranged in the same position they were before.

Ben remarked, "You did a great job, it looks great. I like the way you put everything together."

I said, "Thanks, I did the best I could." We held hands and climbed the stairs to join the children.

"When do you want to open the pub, Norma? We can start tomorrow if you are up to it?"

"Not yet, I am not ready. I need a couple of days to get myself together. I want to spend a few days in the apartment with the kids. They need to settle; this is going to be difficult. I am not ready to face all the customers yet."

Ben replied, "You're right, I need a couple of days, too. It is going to be hard, but let us just keep our chin up and we will be okay."

We also needed that couple of days to become accustomed to being back in the building.

I was pleased at the way the apartment turned out, it looked nice. The ceiling, the walls and the floor had all been replaced; the rooms were painted in a soft, cream color. We had new appliances and our furniture fit perfectly. The smell of smoke had disappeared. There was nothing that reflected that terrible night to remind us of our tragedy.

Yet, sometimes in the night I could still smell the smoke. I would wake up and sit upright in my bed, unable to sleep, and then walk to the children's room where no one was sleeping yet. I would stand there and then walk around the apartment, staring out into the street. The fear and the memories were still there.

The girl's were adamant about not sleeping in their bedroom. They stood there for several minutes as they looked into the room.

Donna said, "Please, Mommy, can we sleep on the sofa bed near you? We don't want to sleep here."

I smiled at her, "Sure, of course you can, your children can sleep wherever you want."

She was happy and replied, "Marty can sleep between me and Trisha." Marty smiled, he liked that. The decision was made. They were scared, especially Donna, who no longer slept without a light on. The girls, having settled their problem, ran outside to play with their friends.

I shouted after them, "Hey, take care of your brother." We had survived the first hurdle of our return.

That night we sat quietly watching the news on television. Suddenly, there was a screeching of tires and a loud crash. We jumped up at the same time and ran to the window. My heart was beating fast.

"What now?" I whispered. We looked out the window into the darkness. Our car was no longer parked in front of the tavern. The street was quiet.

Ben threw open the window and put his head outside.

He said, "Oh my God, someone hit our car. It is wrapped around a telephone pole up the street. Come look."

"Are you kidding?" I replied. I looked out the window and there it was, a mangled mess.

The street was silent; the person had run away, leaving his car with the motor running. Neighbors' lights flickered on and some came out of their homes. Then they turned their attention towards us and shook their heads. The cops never found out who caused the crash. The man who owned the other car claimed it had been stolen. We were fortunate the insurance company repaired our car. This incident just added to the stress we already felt. We never slept in the building at the same time again.

We scheduled a grand opening for the following week. I worried about this evening, not sure if I was ready for a lot of people or the questions that would follow. When I came downstairs, the bar was packed. Art came to bartend. It seemed everyone had dressed up in their finest to make it a special occasion. Some were old customers, many were friends, but there were also many curious strangers. Because there had been so much publicity in the newspapers, they wanted to see Albany Avenue and us. We put on a brave front, trying hard to be cheerful. We ignored any conversation that pertained to the fire and our son.

"Let's not talk about that right now. Everyone is here to enjoy themselves." My customers understood. People were being kind, but it was a tough evening.

Max Weinberg was a very honorable man; a tall, quiet guy who was very shy. He had never married, but liked our company despite the fact we did not have a great deal in common. He lived at the Drake Hotel and was a very private person and our liquor salesmen.

Max worked for Old Rose Liquor Distributors. He was much older than we were. On many occasions he invited Ben and I to have dinner with him. He was a friend. We spent many hours with him where we had wonderful conversations. He had come to our son's wake and his funeral. He was a shoulder I could cry on. When we had the grand opening, he was there.

Maxi, as I called him, said, "Norma I brought my cousin. He is going to help out this evening. My cousin used to do a lot of bartending and could not resist the opportunity to do it again, so I invited him along."

I smiled, "Thanks, I really appreciate all the help we can get."

Max squeezed my hand. His cousin's name was Hymie, a cheerful man who enjoyed conversing with the customers, trying to lighten up the atmosphere. Max told us later that Hymie was Jack Ruby's brother.

Our daughter Diane Theresa was born on September 11, 1965. Ben's mother passed away three days later. I cut my hospital stay short so Ben could leave to attend his mother's funeral.

He said, "Are you sure you will be all right? I hate to leave you with the baby and the bar, what should I do?"

I smiled, "You have only one mother, please go or you will regret it, it is only for a few days. Art is here to help me."

Friends and relatives came and took the children while he was away. My baby stayed with me and we took care of the business. At night, I imagined all sorts of things and was afraid to sleep in the building by myself. I dozed on the couch and waited for morning.

Art was my rock. He helped me each day and without him I probably could not have managed. Diane was a tonic for me and kept me busy. A beautiful child with her curly hair and bright eyes, the girls loved her. Martin was still confused, missing his brother. When Ben returned, we once again put the tavern up for sale, hoping this time it would sell quickly.

Our girls returned to Saint Mathew's School. The angels were still beautifully adorned near the ceiling above the altar. The church arranged for Donna to make her first communion by herself. It would be her special day.

* * *

Note: Hyman Rubenstein was Jack Ruby's brother. Jack had changed his name when he moved to Dallas, Texas. Whether he and Max were also cousins, I really do not know.

CHAPTER 47: LOTS OF TROUBLE

The two years following our return to Albany Avenue were not without incidents. I often wondered how we kept our sanity.

We were soon subjected to the same harassment that the other pubs had endured throughout the years. The police would come into the bar demanding free drinks, making it clear that if we wanted protection we would comply. Many came and went as they pleased. At first we argued, but then found we had become the target of their wrath.

I objected to the fact that when they entered the bar they would walk behind it and help themselves, "What do you think you are doing?" I questioned. "You have no right to come behind the bar. That is why that door is there," I explained, pointing to the half door we had to keep persons from entering behind the bar. They did not say very much to me, but Ben received an earful.

"You know we offer protection. All the other bars, they abide by our rules, and you need to do the same."

Ben protested as well, "Look, this is our bar and I dictate the rules, okay."

Several weeks later, a couple of officers came in. We were busted for serving someone whom they claimed was a minor. We never knew who the person was. The name we received was of someone we did not know.

They explained, "You can either pay us or we will have to turn you in. We can press charges; it is up to you. You know your license will be at stake."

Ben gave them some money. The amount I did not know. They smiled and put the money into their pocket.

"That's how the game is played," one officer said.

"I can't believe you paid them. You know as well as I do we never served anyone underage."

Ben was angry, "Who do we call, Norma, the cops? It is their word against ours. Who do you think will win?" He shrugged his shoulders, "I don't like this any more than you do. I spoke to Harry and Bob from the Venitian Lounge. They said you need to play ball. The police force is corrupt and they pretty much do what they want."

Both of us were unhappy with the situation, but felt we had no choice. The cops pulled several customers out of their cars when leaving the pub and demanded money. They were threatened with jail and drunk driving if they did not pay. If this continued, no one would be willing to come to the tavern and the business would suffer. This was a joke, but we allowed them to come into the bar at will. They drank on or off-duty for free as they wished.

Ben's brother Pat and his wife liked to frequent our place, but every time they did we had an altercation. They always drank too much and Pat was unable to control her. On one occasion when she acted up, Ben tossed her out. In anger, he picked her up with strength he never knew he had. He held her so tight he broke her ribs as he threw her into the taxi. After this incident, we did not see them for a while. But there would be many more of her escapades.

Shortly after that fiasco, Pat with his wife returned with apologies and once again Ben allowed them to stay. By the end of the night, she acted up again. This time she encouraged her son-in-law to start a fight with Ben. He was getting the worst of it when Ben, with a short right, hit him in the stomach, knocking the wind out of him. Pat's wife headed for the phone to call the police.

I headed for her, took the phone cord, and put it around her neck.

"You know," I said, "You give Ben nothing but grief and he doesn't need it. So leave quietly or I will pull this cord so tight you will wish you had." Her eyes bulged out of her head and I released the cord. She left quietly with Pat.

The tavern was not without drama. It was Friday, and payday for most, and one night we had another holdup. Four men came in. Two walked to the back of the pub to check out the bathrooms, making sure they were empty. The other two men took their positions; one in the middle of the bar and one by the front door. He was holding a shotgun.

One man shouted, "Freeze. This is a holdup. Put your hands on your heads, put your faces on the bar and don't move." Everyone, as if programmed, followed instructions.

The men robbed the customers of their jewelry and money. "Hurry," they barked, "Quit stalling."

One man came behind the bar and emptied the cash register. He grabbed bottles of liquor from the back of the bar and threw them against the walls. Shattered glass was everywhere as customers covered their heads, the smell of whiskey filling the air.

From upstairs I could hear the overturning of stools and turned to Ben, "I think there is a fight downstairs."

He listened, "I think you're right. I better get down there fast. Don't come downstairs, I will handle it." Pulling on his clothes he headed down the stairs. As he turned the corner to enter the bar, a gun was pointed at his head.

"Stop right there," the gunman barked. "Don't move. Put your hands on your head."

Collin, a new bartender, was up against the wall, his hands placed on top of his head. There was a gun pointed at his face. He was edgy, but a little vain. Without thinking, he reached into his pocket to pull out a comb to comb his hair. The guy jammed the gun harder into his neck.

He barked, "Don't try that again." Collin's face was ashen as he stood like a statue. We would laugh about this later.

Florena Smith, a heavy-set woman, tried to hide her money in her bra. "That's not smart," he barked in anger. He shoved his hand down her clothes and retrieved the money as he pushed her off the stool. She fell hard onto the floor. He reached down and punched her. Then he kicked another woman with his steel-tipped boots. She had fainted and was lying face down on the ground.

"Stupid bitch," he snarled, as he tore a necklace from her. No one moved, everyone kept their heads down. When the robbery was over, the gunmen backed out of the tavern. They jumped into a car and disappeared into the night, carrying with them an undisclosed amount of money and jewelry. No one was ever caught or charged. Sometime later we were told the cops thought one of the robbers was an ex-policeman.

On a quiet night during the week, several men on motorcycles entered the pub. Ben watched them carefully. Soon they became involved with the locals in a pool competition. The locals accused the men of cheating. All hell broke loose as they began hitting each other over the head with pool cues. Ben got into the thick of things, trying to break up the fight.

As he went to pick up one of the men to explain, "We do not want any trouble here," the man pulled out a knife and began carving up his body.

He did not feel the deep gash in his arm, as the blade was sharp. He was aware of the cut and watched the blood as it oozed from his arm, then realized the blood on his shirt was coming from his stomach. As he put his hand up to thrust the knife away, his hand touched the blood from his neck and back.

Ben said, "Hey man. I am trying to help you. What the hell are you doing?" When he looked around, he realized he was alone in the bar. The customers who started the fight had locked themselves in the bathroom. The motorcycle boys backed out the door. With their knives still in their hands, they rode off into the night. The guy with the shiv gave Ben a salute as he left. He said, "I am sorry."

Ben raced upstairs shouting. He stopped short at the living room entrance, worried that the blood would drip onto the carpet. I came out of the bedroom still half asleep.

"What is wrong?" I asked. The sight of him caught me by surprise, "Oh my God." My screams woke the children who looked at their father in horror. "What happened?"

He said, "I will explain later. Take me to the hospital. I need stitches." His arm was severed near the elbow, the blood soaking the floor. His shirt, now in tatters, was a deep crimson color.

I quickly tied a towel around his body then wrapped a rag around his arm, trying to stem the flow of blood.

"God, Ben you are losing a lot of blood. We need to get to the hospital." To the girls I said, "Daddy will be okay. I will call Stacy to take care of you, don't worry." I hugged them and felt them trembling. "It is going to be all right," I assured them. The situation was urgent and I knew it was imperative that I get him to the hospital quickly before he collapsed. Grabbing my purse, we rapidly descended the stairs.

I told the idiot pool players to leave and was not interested in their explanations, calling them a bunch of cowards.

I said to Stacy who was appalled, "Please watch the kids, Art will be here soon." I locked the door and then quickly hurried in the direction of the emergency room. Ben received sixty stitches and needed a blood transfusion. He refused to stay overnight. The next day the men were full of apologies.

A number of weeks later, a scuffle broke out between several of the boys playing pool. The men had been drinking heavily. Ben hurried around the bar to break up the fight. One man fell between the jukebox and the wall. As Ben tried to pick him up another guy jumped on his back.

I watched apprehensively from behind the bar, then thought, "What the hell." I was still angry because of the last incident on the pool table; therefore I reached for the blackjack under the counter. I slipped it up the sleeve of my sweater and hurried towards the jukebox. I tried to pull the guy off his back, but could not, so I took the blackjack and thumped the fellow on the head. I tried to whack him lightly, but it was a pretty hard strike.

He fell on the floor, holding his head, "Who the hell hit me?" he cried out. I quickly returned to stand behind the bar. Ben got up; the fight was over.

The next day, the guy I had struck on the head came in for a drink. I was glad he was okay, but he had a pretty good lump on his head. He said, "I couldn't make work today. Someone hit me last night, see the egg I have."

I smiled "You shouldn't be fighting, that's what happens when you don't behave." He never knew that I was the one, but we had to protect each other with whatever it took.

Family should be supportive. Pat and his wife returned and once again she was like Jekyll and Hyde. Ben sighed as he pulled Pat aside.

"I hope you two can behave yourselves this time. We don't need any trouble here." He glanced over his shoulder and noticed she was already ordering drinks.

"Both of you drink too much. Maybe you should not drink. That way you can keep an eye on her."

Pat nodded his head, "Sorry, Ben, she said she would not cause any trouble."

Sober, his wife was a gem. With a drink, she was something

else and after a few drinks intolerable. Thank God neither of them drove a car, and taxis were their means of transportation.

At closing time, she refused to leave. Pat was trying his best to remove her physically. "Come on, Ben needs to close. The taxi is here."

Pat was a chap who was too easygoing. They had no children and little responsibility. Life been had been a party. Both drank too much. She was belligerent and refused to move off the stool. Suddenly, she lifted her glass and threw it at Ben, who was standing by the register. The glass shattered as it hit the floor.

Ben jumped out of harm's way, "What the hell," he said angrily, "What is wrong with you? You need to get a hold of her."

I was sitting at the end of the bar and jumped up quickly. Running along the top of the bar, I knocked her onto the floor as I leaped off the counter. Taking off my high-heel, shoes I began beating her.

Ben pulled me off. "Stop it, Norma, what are you doing? You don't want to hurt her." I looked at him, there had been so much frustration building up in me, I was losing it. What had happened to all the diplomacy I use to have?

One evening we decided to go out for dinner. I was disappointed when our sitter did not show. We debated whether to go or not, even though we were dressed and ready.

Ben said, "Come on. I promised to take you to dinner. We'll only be gone for an hour." Bernie promised to check on the children.

"Go ahead," Bernie said, "I'll take care of things. You will not be gone that long." Ben was concerned as many customers filtered into the bar that it was going to be a busy night. I was a bit dubious if he could handle it. Bernie was another bricklayer keen to earn extra money, so Ben gave him the opportunity.

They had worked together as bricklayers and had known each

other for several years. Bernie liked to be noticed and standing behind a bar he would have everyone's undivided attention. We were reluctant to leave him, as this was his first night working in the pub. Ben spoke to some regulars who said they were more than happy to assist if there was any trouble.

He was average height, slim and not attractive, a Scotsman who lost his brogue quickly. He spoke with a fake American accent, trying to fit in. Bernie was fearful of men who were rough and ready and was not a guy who liked fighting if required. I felt he was not good material for a bartender; if a scuffle occurred, I don't know what he would do. Neither Ben nor I thought he would work out.

I said, "He is too nervous for the bar. If the customers don't respect him, they will make his life miserable."

Ben agreed, "Yeah, I wonder how long he will last?"

We returned in less than two hours, neither one of us had felt comfortable leaving the children without a sitter. Upon our return, I hastened upstairs to change my clothes. I noticed the dresser in disarray and the safe door wide open. The safe was empty. Had I forgotten to lock it? I glanced back to the dresser and the entire contents of our jewelry box were gone. Baffled, I ran downstairs and called Ben to the side. He looked at me in disbelief and together we went upstairs.

He said, "Who was up here?" I shook my head and looked at the children sound asleep on the sofa bed. Thank God, they were safe. Ben went downstairs to confront Bernie, who was not aware of what happened.

Bernie evidently did not notice that someone had slipped upstairs. Customers said he was too engrossed in chatting up a couple of girls, instead of paying attention to the job at hand.

They also said, "We could hardly get a drink. He was too busy with the females." While he was *too busy*, our house was robbed. Our daughters told us later that they saw a man but pretended to be asleep. They were scared. Ben tried to control his anger.

Bernie's casual manner irked me, mostly because anything could have happened to the children. The police were called to conduct an investigation.

Bernie was first to say, "Gosh, Ben, I couldn't handle the bar. These guys are a pretty rough bunch. I didn't think it would be this busy." He tried to make light of the incident, copping a plea and shrugging his shoulders.

I looked at Bernie with distaste. It is easy to make excuses for yourself and it's easy to walk away as long as its not you at the receiving end.

I turned to Ben and asked, "Why do we always trust people? Why do we never go with our gut feeling? We both knew he would not work out."

Ben replied, "I thought he could handle it for a couple of hours."

Several days later, the police returned. The officers and we both knew who the thief was. Florena Smith, a customer for several years, recently had a wayward son visit her. She came from the South, a woman who enjoyed her drink and younger men.

It was common knowledge that Florena (Flo) Smith had children by many different fathers. Some we knew, others we had never met. This particular son recently put an appearance in town, a dirty, shifty character who did not like to work. His jet-black hair and straggly beard were unkempt. He often hung around the pub, soliciting drinks.

Ben mentioned, "He is worth keeping an eye on. I dislike men who come into a bar broke and prey on others. Most of these guys are pretty good hearted."

Old Mrs. Smith was distraught and said she could not believe her son would do something like that in a place she frequented. "Oh Lord," she said, "I am so sorry. He has always been a drifter and never was up to much good."

The police officers alleged that Smith was bound for California where he had a brother.

One officer said "We will do this on our own time, but first we will need the fare and some money for expenses. We will bring him back." The officers had it all figured out. They assured us of their intentions and were pleased with themselves. They were no better than Smith, just another shakedown, looking for a free vacation at our expense.

I looked at them in disgust, "Look, why don't we just forget it?"

In the days that followed, a feeling of helplessness engulfed me. When Ben left for work, I was on my own. No one entered the bar unless I recognized them. Art came each day to help out at lunchtime. Our lives were in such turmoil. Anxiety filled my heart and I felt we would be here forever. Every day I woke with a heavy heart, wondering what was going to happen next.

CHAPTER 48: BOB'S MOTEL

In the spring of 1967, the tavern sold. I reckon it was one of the happiest days of my life. Unfortunately, in less than a year we would get the tavern back. The new owners, who were Cubans, lost their license and could not pay the mortgage. One of the men was a citizen the other was not. After an argument, the one who held the license left. Because of this, the tavern was returned to us. We eventually sold it to an insurance company who paid us several thousand dollars and were willing to take over the mortgage.

Because of the Chicago weather, the building trade never guaranteed steady work. One day as I read the classified section of the newspaper, I thought, *A motel might be an interesting business.*

"Come," I said, "We will have to move soon. Let's look at these motels listed in the paper and see what we think." We piled all the kids in the car as if it were an adventure. We traveled the entire length of Illinois and looked at several motels. All of them took us further away from Chicago.

Ben said, "These places are too far away. I don't want to be this far from the city; what do you think?" I felt the same. Both of us wanted to be near our son.

On our travels, we found Bob's Motel at 9117 Indianapolis Boulevard, Highland, Indiana, commonly known as Highway 41. The location of the motel was thirty miles south of Chicago in Indiana, close enough to visit our son and far enough away from our past life. This was our opportunity to start over again. It seemed like a safe business. We were energized and the children loved the prospect of moving.

The kids were excited with their new surroundings. There would be a new school and new friends. For us, it was a new business in which we had no experience, so we had a lot to learn. The buildings were old and in need of a lot of repair.

Ben was restless and drove to Chicago on many occasions. It was as if he could not let go of the past. His favorite place was the Venetian Lounge, where he met with old friends and old customers. Bob Frawley and Harry Julian, owners of the Venetian Lounge, were always glad to see him.

Kidding, Bob said, "We have missed you, Ben, and it would be nice if you could just sing us a few songs."

Ben laughed as they gave each other a hug. Bob also worked for Midwest Fence, but had teamed up with Harry in the bar business several years before.

Late one evening, while Ben was at the Venetian Lounge, Sal, a friend of Sam's, approached him. "I don't like the fact that you helped put one of our friends in prison. I heard you refused to testify for Sam. This does not sit well with me and my friends." He gestured to some guys sitting in the corner.

When Ben did not respond he added, "By the way, you didn't move far enough away. We know where you live." He cursed loudly with threats to get even.

Sal was a small, bald man who tried to portray an air of decency when he frequented our place. He was a guy who liked to dress in suits as his job required. He and Chuck were old friends and did a lot of whispering together. He was employed by the City and Chuck informed us he was a stand-up guy, whatever that meant. Sam DeStefano had many connections, which reached far into city hall. I can say in all honesty that he probably got Sal the job.

Bob, the bartender that night, stepped in to put a stop to his outburst. He said, "That's enough. You're drunk; it is time to go home. We don't need that kind of talk here." It was near closing time.

Ben had not spoken yet, but responded, "Look, it is late and Bob wants to close. Next Friday night I will meet you here around eight and we can talk."

Sal snarled, "Yea, I'll be here." Bob continued to clear the bar. He was listening intently to the conversation and kept an eye on Sal's movements.

After he left, Bob smiled and said, "I will be here, too. You always have a backup, Ben." I am sure they also had a gun behind the bar somewhere.

I was apprehensive when Ben related the incident to me.

"Look, let's not get involved with these people. They are dangerous."

But the following Friday night, he was ready to drive to Chicago. Ben said, "Don't worry, I'll be back." He put the gun in his car under the seat and added, "They are not coming out here. If there is trouble I will make sure I take one of them with me."

"This is not a joke, don't talk like that. This is serious. I do not want you to go. Please don't go. You know what these people are capable of. Haven't we been through enough? God knows what could happen to you."

"Look, I have to go, Norma. I can't stay here and wait to see if they show up. They know where we live. I can't take that chance." Ben kissed my cheek and I clung to him. "You worry too much, I will be fine."

He jumped into his car and I watched as he drove off. I paced up and down the entire night and finally sold my last room and waited. Usually I went to bed, but was too upset to sleep. I began to doze, curled up on the sofa. In the early hours of the morning, I heard his car turn into the driveway. Relieved and concerned, I ran out to greet him.

"I have been so worried, what happened?" He took my arm as we walked together into the house.

"You are shaking," he said, pulling me close to him. "Would you believe they did not show up? Bob and I were waiting for them. And guess what, I was stopped by a traffic cop for speeding, but he let me go with a warning. I was concerned because I had the gun under the seat. I was late arriving and thought I had missed them, but Bob said no one had come. I stayed until closing time then hung around in case they were outside waiting to ambush me. Bob walked me to my car, but no one was around, so I left." We never saw or heard from Sal again.

Fear is a terrible thing. It takes over your life. I was not sleeping well and worried constantly, imagining all the terrible things that could happen. Ben worried as well; the visits to Chicago became less frequent. He decided to stay closer to home. He still liked to meet people and became bored with the motel. We were trying hard to put our lives back together, but it was difficult.

I once said there was a downside to every business and the motel was no exception. It was not without controversy and there were many incidents. Customers would steal bedding or towels. The television sets had to be bolted to the dressers. We would have disputes between couples that lived in the efficiencies. Once again, we had to be diplomatic. Dogs were not allowed in the rooms. Many times we would find a dog belonging to the renter tied up outside their window. One morning, the maid found a man who committed suicide with a shotgun in room #7. It was an unnerving experience.

Often anonymous husbands or wives would drive around the premises. They would be checking to see if their spouses were in any of the rooms with someone else. There was a woman who was distraught after she had lost her children in a fire. I had booked her in the last room, room #38. The room was located next to the highway.

She left her room and wandered onto Highway 41where she was killed by a car. Her body was thrown into the air, crushed beyond recognition. I cried for her and her children.

CHAPTER 49: LAWSUIT

In the weeks that followed, no other incidents occurred that were related to Sam. To our knowledge, he was in prison. Chuck's whereabouts were of no concern to us. Ben seldom went to Chicago.

J.C.'s wife, decided to sue us for a large amount of money for J.C.'s death, under workman's compensation. Other than our visits to the cemetery, these were our only visits to Chicago. Her attorney would summon us to his office where we were subjected to going over the crime scene several times. Every time, we reviewed pictures of the fire where the bodies laid and it haunted us. It may not have disturbed Judy but it took us days to wipe the images from our minds. Each time after leaving his office, I broke down and cried. Ben was visibly upset and stared at her with hate in his heart.

"What makes her so cold and heartless, she is a despicable woman." Most times he wanted to stop by the Venetian Lounge. He felt a kinship there and felt the need for a drink surrounded by familiar faces that cared about us. Because I was upset, I waited in the car. In the end, I would drive home.

The hearings were constantly postponed for reasons that were unknown to us. Ben felt we had been through enough and refused to settle. We believed that she was not entitled to compensation as J.C. had only worked for four hours each week, but for us this was not the issue. We believed that both J.C. and our dear son were victims of arson, the callous actions of cold-hearted criminals. We grieved for J.C also, but the fire was not our fault. We had willingly paid for the funeral expenses, a trust fund had been created for the children, plus she had received a settlement from Midwest Fence.

The effects of these visits took their toll on us. Each one left me traumatized and exhausted. The pictures were very graphic, outlining where our son had died and where J.C. was found. I hated her because she was so nonchalant about the whole thing. The photos did not appear to bother her when she looked at them. Her attorney was very persistent and we wondered if this would ever end.

Several years passed, each time old wounds were reopened. In the summer of 1969, Ben went to Scotland to visit his family; his father was up in years. When our attorney Bill Glass called and wanted to schedule a meeting, I met him myself because Ben was out of the country.

The case was becoming a headache for Bill. We had been stubborn, taking up precious time because we refused to settle. The amount had become significantly less as time went on.

When Bill arrived at the motel that evening, he appeared agitated. "That's a long drive. I should have come in the daytime, but I wanted to avoid the traffic." He paused, "I am out of breath and haven't even asked how you are. Where is Ben?" He grabbed me roughly and hugged me, planting a kiss on my check. "You look well, the motel must agree with you."

I smiled; somehow the same feelings of trust and affection were no longer present. I responded without warmth, "I am well and Ben has gone to Scotland to visit his father. You and I can discuss the case ourselves."

He agreed and I continued, "You know I am tired of this ridiculous situation. Do you know how many years this has been going on? It is a travesty and has to come to an end. Lets get to the point, what amount of money are they looking for, now?"

He was jovial and liked my response, rubbing his hands together. "That's the way to go." He grinned, "Look we can settle for $5,000, it's a hell of a lot less than the $20,000 they started with." He paused,

"You are doing the right thing."

I smiled at him, "I am glad you think so. I would have preferred not to settle, but to review those photos again is too painful." We talked for a little while about nothing. I could see he was anxious to leave. I gave him the $5,000. He wanted half by check and half in cash. I am not sure who got the cash and did not know if J.C.'s wife received anything. Somehow. I did not care.

Ben was angry because he did not want to settle. "I am sorry, but I cannot view those pictures any longer. I am sick of watching you punish yourself. It takes days to erase those photos from our minds. This is destroying us," I said, "Can't you see that?"

Ben coped by drinking too much. It was not a solution. He was drinking too much after the fire and was doing the same thing now. The $5,000 dollars was the answer. It was a small price to pay for our sanity. We never saw Bill again.

CHAPTER 50: NEW BUSINESS

Sean Edward, the Edward after my father, was born in 1969. Martin was excited.

He said, "I am glad I have a brother. I hate all these girls around me. They're bossy." I guess he had felt outnumbered.

The five years had passed quickly since Benny's death. It still haunted us, but we did not talk about it. We were happier than we had been for some time. The children appeared to have settled down in their new environment and had many friends. They liked their new school and began to participate in lots of activities. Martin liked baseball, and the girls became involved in dance and acrobatics.

The motel covered approximately an acre of land. We had thirty-eight one-story units that were built around the house. On one side there were efficiencies and rooms for truckers, on the other side and at the back were our better rooms. These rooms were carpeted and more luxurious and were usually reserved for tourists and couples. It was a nice setup and the motel did well. The fear we had felt for such a long time was slowly disappearing. We thought we were in a safer environment.

I loved the motel and threw myself into the business. It was hard work. I enjoyed remaking the rooms in soft colors and decorated each room with pride. My daughter Trisha had a flair for color and style and liked to assist me. We spent hours together working on the rooms, painting every room in a ray of pastel colors with new matching carpet. The rooms were seductive.

The outside of the motel was painted a soft pink, the doors and windows trimmed in a dark wine color, making the motel more appealing. Every night our rooms were filled. It also became a practice that our steady customers, when finished with the room, would either call on the phone or drop their key off at the office. This way we could clean and the rent the room again. It was a very lucrative business.

On the north side of the motel, the last six rooms had garages attached to them. Many repeat customers who liked seclusion appreciated this. They could put their automobile in the garage and have privacy. Our motel was popular. We were cordial with our clientele. The customers filled out a registration card and there was not too much communication, just friendly conversations.

The house was a two-story building that stood in the center of the property. A laundry room was at the back of the building and an office at the front; both attached to our living quarters. When you came out of the living room you were in the office. The mirrors were situated where one could see the customers as they approached the office door before entering.

Ben did not enjoy the motel business as much as I did. He was restless.

"This is woman's work," he remarked. "I am picking up my tools again and going to work. I saw a bricklaying job up the street and spoke to the guy. He hired me."

I was happy for him. After we painted and cleaned the motel, there were not many things he could do. He definitely did not relish repair work. His Chicago visits were less frequent and soon he found a new place to hang out. It was a nightclub on Highway 41.

He said," I am just up the street if you need me." Mr. Kenny's had a small motel facing the highway and behind it was a restaurant and bar. They had a band, which played on weekends. Ben liked to sing with the band. He soon earned a reputation in the area as someone who could sing all the good old songs and give a first-class performance. They loved him at the pub. He did not get paid and the pub received free entertainment.

We had dinner at Mr. Kenny's several times. Ben knew everyone and was in his element. People made requests for songs and he sang them. On one occasion, while at dinner, he hoped onto the stage and sang a song to me. I sighed and said, "It's all very well, Ben, it would be nice if you were paid. Mr. Kenny is doing fine with free entertainment." But that was Ben and no one was going to change him.

The highlight of each year was New Year's Eve. Because we had the kids and the business, we could not go anywhere. We decided we would celebrate New Year's at the motel and invited many couples we knew from Chicago. It was an ideal situation.

BERNARD MCCLUSKIE

CHAPTER 51: MORE CORRUPTION

To our knowledge, Sam was spending time in prison. Someone told us that he had applied for parole, but was denied. In 1969, the book *Captive City* was published and some friends brought it to our attention. The book was about Chicago and the Mafia. It portrayed the ugly side of the city and the prevalence of organized crime. The story of the fire and us were in the book. I resented the manner in which we were portrayed, which indicated we were friendly with Sam. The facts were incorrect and insulting.

Many stories about Sam have been told in newspapers, on television or on the news. Documentaries have appeared on crime channels. The same cast of characters that were mentioned in the book came from articles that were on file in the State's Attorney Office. From the many sources, I have tried to put together what I have read so each person can understand the kind of people we are dealing with.

Many collectors worked for Sam, one story was about another character, Peter Cappilletti. Sam believed Peter was withholding money from him. Peter was invited to Sam's brother's restaurant where they lured him into the basement. Several men were present and Peter was chained naked to a hot radiator and beaten. Everyone, including Chuck, took turns urinating on the man to humiliate him further. This act was carried out in the presence of his wife.

Both Sam and Chuck loved the power of guns and were capable of murder. Putting a gun to a man's head just to hear him cry and beg thrilled them. The disgusting use of profanities in front of the man's family brought them laughter. Constant threats to tear a man's eyes out with an ice-pick, and the use of a cigarette to burn a person, delighted them. Sam drooled over his victims, his mouth twisted in a sadistic manner. The spit would run down his face. Both men took pleasure in kicking a man when he was down. They relished their supremacy as they listened to his screams. Chuck was no different than Sam, an eager participant.

I had met Charles Siragusa briefly, but after reading the book, many things fell into place. The book spoke about Charles Siragusa, who was brought in from New York. He became head of the Illinois Crime Investigating Commission. His job was to help clean up organized crime in the city of Chicago. DeStefano was one of his top priorities. During his investigations, he also came across our file and decided to pursue it. He began by investigating alleged accusations of corrupt officials. There was an impressive list of these officials, such as assistant prosecutors, defense attorneys, police captains and judges.

One of the judges on the list he was investigating was Cecil Smith. He had been a judge since 1932. It was alleged that he took bribes to fix several cases. He resigned in 1964. He was one of Sam's judges and frequented his home. In Judge Smith's court one day, Sam refused to pay a ten-dollar fine for going down a one-way street. He insisted on a trial and would serve as his own attorney. He taunted the judge and made a fool of the court procedures. Before the court, he waved a handful of thousand dollar bills.

"Who says it's wrong to have money?" Sam overturned a glass of water and began wiping the floor with his bill exclaiming, "I have a million dollars and am wiping up your stinking courtroom." The whole procedure became a spectacle.

The frequent courtroom disruptions by Sam were the worst the Chicago Crime Commission had ever seen. Sam took advantage of his status in the outfit and his popularity in the gossip columns. He loved an audience and people came to his trials to witness his antics, which were very theatrical.

When Sam was charged with illegal voting, he arrived at the courtroom on a stretcher dressed in a red silk gown over pajamas. He roared profanities through a bullhorn as he went down the hallway of the court building. He insulted every official in charge. Charles Siragusa was the man who had initiated the court procedures. Sam referred to him as stool pigeon. The proceedings were held in Judge Daniel Ryan's courtroom. Sam was discourteous to the judge. Judge Ryan decided to continue the court case another day. He was accused of giving DeStefano preferential treatment, which he denied. He explained that it was better to get Sam out of his courtroom.

"I have dealt with DeStefano before and I am not going to play into his hands by acknowledging his antics."

When we heard or read articles about Sam, it seemed a world away. We did not dwell on the past even though the past was always there to haunt us.

CHAPTER 52: ANOTHER HOLD UP

It was on Monday, May 11, 1970, a day after Mother's Day
. Sean had a high fever that day. I waited for Ben to come home from
his job so I could take him to a clinic, which was open late in the
evening. He took care of the office.

When I returned, I said, "Wow, you have been busy." Most of
the rooms were sold. "I am going to have an early night," I remarked
glancing at the keyboard.

"Yeah, it was a good night, lots of truckers." Outside, the lot
was crowded; the big trucks obscuring our vision to the highway.

It was near 11:00 PM when a man walked up to the office from
out of nowhere. I saw him in the mirror and wondered where he
had come from. He seemed to emerge from the shadows. He did
not drive into the motel, therefore I thought perhaps he was already
booked and needed some assistance.

He was a tall, black man; a cap sat on the top of a large Afro
hairdo, a stranger who appeared nervous. He looked around, making
sure we were alone as he peered into the living room. His actions
were conspicuous, but since he was a new customer in unfamiliar
territory, it did not occur to me to feel threatened. Not many black
people came to the motel. Most that did had been coming for years
and were known to me.

I smiled, "Can I help you."

"Yeah," he said, "I need a room. How much are they?" I glanced
at the keyboard to see what was available, afraid to turn him down.

Because of the uprisings that had been taking place, I did not want him to think I was a racist. Once again, I wondered where his car was. Usually customers drove up to the motel and parked under the carport in full view.

I asked, "Is the room for one or two?" He did not respond. I quoted a price for two persons.

When a customer came into the office it was customary to hand them a registration form to fill out. He took it in his hand, staring intently at me as he accepted a pen to write down the details. Instead of standing in front of me, he suddenly shifted to the side of the desk. I became uneasy as I watched him scribble some information on the registration card. He handed it back to me but nothing he had written made sense. The information was in the wrong places. His name was a scrawl; the city of Hammond and Gary were printed all over the place. No license plate number appeared on the card, plus he did not fill out how many people would occupy the room. I had a gut feeling something was wrong. He was standing so near to me that I could hear his shallow breathing and his presence was frightening. I was not accustomed to a customer being this close.

As I glanced up, still holding the card, my eyes became level with his hands. I was startled to see a gun aimed directly at my face. He was tall. My heart began to beat rapidly, I was afraid to look up, telling myself not to panic. I took a step backwards and sat down quickly behind the desk. Backing my chair into the corner of the wall, I let my body cover the window behind me where Sean was sleeping. I looked at the man's face. His piercing dark eyes were staring at me as he smiled. My heart was pounding. I was terrified. My mind raced, wondering what my next move should be. I thought about the gun we had. It was locked above me in the cupboard.

I lowered my eyes, stared at the desk and in a quiet voice said, "Take what you want," then threw open the cash drawer.

He laughed out loud, still staring, still smiling. Suddenly, without hesitation, he fired the gun. The bullet struck me in the face.

It entered the corner of my lip into my mouth, shattering the bones on the left side of my jaw. There was a burning sensation as dark red blood began spilling out of my mouth. Pieces of my teeth fell onto the desk. The blood spattered onto my papers. I looked up at him in horror and watched as he turned and ran out the door.

Many thoughts entered my mind, "Oh my God, I've been shot. I think I am okay."

I put my hands up to my face, touching the red, sticky substance. I stared at my hands in shock. Large, dark-scarlet drops fell onto my clothing and floor as the blood oozed out of my mouth.

"Don't come out here, I have been shot." In a state of shock I tried to pick up the fragments of my teeth. I could not sit down and began to panic.

Ben heard the gun shot and came running out of the living room. He stared at me, then ran back into the house bringing a towel, "Oh my God, hold this up to your face," he cried out.

He turned and chased the man. The gunman jumped into a waiting car parked up front between the large trucks. The car took off onto Highway 41, disappearing into the night.

Ben grabbed the phone from me as I was trying to call for help. "What are you doing?" "My wife has been shot," he screamed. Frantically, he began cleaning up the desk and floor, throwing my papers into the trashcan. Blood was everywhere.

"You need to sit still while we a wait for the ambulance," he said. "Every time you jump around it causes more bleeding."

One officer told us it was a Dum-dum bullet. This type of bullet was soft-nosed or hollow point. It was a bullet that expanded on impact.

The police and the ambulance came and whisked me away to the nearest hospital. Ben reached out to Blanche, a lady who worked at the motel, to come and help him.

"Norma has been shot. Can you please come and watch the kids, and hurry."

"I will be there as fast as I can. Oh, Lord." Blanche Barnett and I became friends when we first came to the motel. She was a lady in her 50s from Mississippi. Having worked at the motel for years, she was instrumental in teaching us about the motel business. It was a friendship that lasted for over forty years until she died in 2007 at the age of 92.

The paramedics rushed me into surgery. My jawbone was crushed. The surgeons cleaned the wound and wired my shattered bones together.

I was semi-conscious when I returned to my room, feeling dazed and shaky from the medication. My mind was somewhat alert and I felt the need to see myself. The horror on Ben's face spoke volumes as he held my hand without conviction. He stared at me and I saw he had been crying.

"You are going to be fine," he said. I tried to smile. "Just rest, I will be back. I need to check on the kids and let Blanche go home." He bent down and kissed me on the top of my head. I closed my eyes.

After he left, no one was in sight. I lay in my bed for several minutes feeling groggy as the medication began taking effect. My eyes were bleary, but with sheer determination I pulled myself out of bed. I held onto the walls and walked slowly, following the light to the bathroom. My legs were unsteady, but I was determined as I stumbled into the space directly in front of the sink. I raised my head to look into the mirror. My body swayed as I leaned against the sink trying to position myself. I looked up into the glass and I thought I was seeing double.

I was horrified and uttered a silent cry, "Oh my God." The tears spilled down my cheeks. I stood and stared for what seemed an eternity and whispered to myself, "Is that you?" A big, black, swollen face stared back at me. I raised my hand and touched my cheek; it was numb. No wonder Ben looked at me in horror.

***

The nuns from the children's school kneeled around my bed reciting the rosary. I tried to smile as I lifted my hands to my face feeling the thick bandages.

They smiled, then handed me many wonderful cards from the children at Our Lady of Grace School. "Our prayers are answered. The whole school is praying for you."

We thought the children heard nothing. They were used to the noise at the motel. Trisha recalled that she had heard the sirens, but went back to sleep. She said, "I prayed it had nothing to do with us."

Donna was first to wake up that morning and came down stairs looking for me. Sensing the confusion, she asked her father what was going on. He explained that a gunman had shot me, but the doctor said I would have a full recovery.

"I have been to the hospital and Mom is okay, she had surgery last night."

She ran upstairs, "Trisha, Trisha wake up. Mommy has been shot, but Dad says she is going to be okay. She is in the hospital," The girls were excited and distraught at the same time, holding each other as they cried. Because of our history, the police in this small town were concerned. Lieutenant Horner posted a guard at my door. There was no end to what Sam could do. I tried to play it down to the cops, worrying that Sam might send someone else. It could have been one of our daughters. They often answered the switchboard or were at the desk. It was a chilling thought.

Lieutenant Horner took my statement. He said, "I am your neighbor. I live just behind the motel. Please call me night or day if you need me." He sensed I was frightened and was concerned. He stopped by every day to monitor my progress. I was grateful for his concern. After my release from the hospital, the Lieutenant and I went to the next town, Gary to look at mug shots. There were hundreds of files of known criminals.

"Go through these files and see if you can identify the man." Several hours later, I informed him that I could not recognize him. He was never found; but I knew this had something to do with Sam. The police thought so too. The money was in plain view and had not been taken.

BOB'S MOTEL, HIGHLAND, INDIANA

BOB'S MOTEL

-onian
May-1976
Wounded

HIGHLAND — The wife of the owner of Bob's Motel, 9117 Indianapolis Blvd., was shot in the face at point-blank range in a robbery attempt Monday night.

Mrs. Norma McCluskey is in fair condition in St. Margaret Hospital. Officials said the slug from the small caliber pistol struck the woman in the mouth and came out her cheek.

The holdup occurred...
man
polic
her

WOMAN SHOT IN HIGHLAND, INDIANA

209

The gunman had one thing in mind and that was to shoot me.

Eating and drinking through a straw was difficult with my mouth wired shut, but it was preferable to being fed through a tube in my nose. My face was somewhat painful, but pain pills helped and my discomfort was tolerable. When most of the swelling was gone and the bruising disappeared, I felt better.

The first surgery was a failure. It was disappointing when the wires were removed and my jaw fell. My mouth hung down to one side.

The doctor was optimistic, "Never mind," he said, "We will try something else." Another surgery was scheduled.

Ben's father was coming for a visit. It was an inconvenient time, but we did not want to alarm him. I said, "It is all right. He can stay upstairs in your room and the girls will help me." He was horrified at what had happened, but was most gracious throughout his stay.

CHAPTER 53: SURGERIES AND RECOVERY

I went through four surgeries. The second one used a plastic bone that was grafted into my face. The plastic was a substitute for a jawbone but it became apparent that plastic was not the answer. Once again, my jaw collapsed. My mouth was still in the wrong place.

My next two surgeries were in Chicago and more successful. Some bullet fragments in my neck could not be removed. There was a permanent scar where the path of the bullet tore a nerve from the corner of my mouth to the side of my chin. It was a deep, ugly line leaving that part of my face numb. After scores of X-rays, Doctor Rockwell was ready to perform the third surgery. As I sat in his office waiting for my turn, I noticed the severity of the other patients' injuries. Several children had no palates in their mouths. One lady had no ear, and there were men and women who had been in car accidents, their faces distorted where nerves had been severed. I remember thinking, *You don't look so bad. Lots of people are worse off than you.*

The third operation took seven hours, but was successful. A bone removed from my hip was used as a jawbone. Several weeks later, the day arrived to remove the bandages. The nurse smiled at me as she worked skillfully with her small scissors.

She understood my apprehension. "Come," she smiled, "You are going to love the result. Look in the mirror. Your face looks excellent; after all, Doctor Rockwell is the best."

I lifted my head gradually and looked in the mirror. What an unexpected thrill I received. My mouth was in the right place, no bruises or swelling as in my previous surgeries. It was overwhelming. The tears came.

We hugged each other, "Thank you so much."

She chuckled, "Don't thank me; you need to thank Doctor Rockwell."

Smiling, I said, "Now all I need is teeth."

CHAPTER 54: PRECAUTIONS

Shortly after the third surgery I was pregnant again. James Christopher, named after J.C., was born on November 22, 1971. I was tired; tired of hospitals, tired of the turmoil happening all around us. With a new baby and the children, I decided not to have the plastic surgery that Doctor Rockwell recommended. He had hoped to cover the scars by doing skin grafting from the back of my neck.

He said, "I understand, but one more surgery is essential to remove the scar tissue from the inside of your mouth. We need to do this so you can have dentures made."

"I know," I replied, "but I need to make arrangements for someone to take care of the baby. He is so small; who will take care of him? He is only five months old."

While in Chicago one day, Ben stopped at Pat's home and explained about my surgeries Pat's wife said, "I will care for him. I love babies." She was excited. Ben was confident, "If she is sober, she will be great with the baby. She won't be going anywhere. I will check every day. They never drink in the house. They only go out on weekends."

I responded uneasily, "I hope so."

He replied, "It's only for a couple of days." I was not totally convinced, but James was fine. I guess everyone has some good qualities.

In order to reduce the need for direct contact with the customers, Ben built a wall of concrete blocks that began in the basement and extended to the office ceiling. He then inserted a bulletproof window and steel bars were installed on the downstairs windows. When I did rooms at night, the gun came with me. Ben watched me from the doors of the house as I walked to the room reaching my destination. When the unit was cleaned and rentable; a phone call alerted him to stand at the door. He watched me walk back to the house safely. Our way of life had become very different. The children were not allowed to venture far and were driven everywhere they wanted to go: to a friend's house, to school or a sports event. Bicycles were out now. Regrettably, the strain was getting to us.

Two years passed, but in the summer of 1972 I finally had new dentures. To me, they were perfect. I wore wigs for a while as my hair continued to fall out, but I felt almost normal.

CHAPTER 55: THE FRENCH LINE

In August of 1972, Ben planned a vacation to Scotland to see his father who was at this time in his 80s. Subsequently, a decision was made that all of us would go.

Having saved some money over the years, he said, "Look, we only live once. We can drive to New York, take our car and book a trip on a ship going to the U.K. Lets travel to Scotland in style. With the car, we will have our own transportation. Let's make a real vacation out of it. We have the money, let's spend it, life is short." We purchased a new car and then booked our trip and made our plans. I was very excited; it had been a tough two years.

This was not my first visit to Scotland. We took our first holiday to Scotland in January 1962. I had spent weeks in preparation, outfitting the girls in beautiful new coats, bonnets and dresses. Benny had his first pair of long pants and wanted to wear the red jacket I had bought him for Easter with his red top hat. He liked to dress up in nice clothes, like his father. Marty was only six months old and not aware of what was going on. I thought, *Lots of warm pajamas for you, my young man.* Scotland's climate was bitter and damp. Ben's parents had met the girls a few years earlier on a visit to the State's, but had not met our sons.

Ben was well known in his hometown and people came from near and far to see him. As a teenager, he loved the dance halls and learned every dance he could. The crowd would give him space to perform as he went into his routine, loving the attention he received. He had a love for music and could sing, but his first love was the game of soccer, where at one point he had hoped to become a professional. But having to serve two years in Germany as required by the British Government ended that dream. He served an apprenticeship as a mason when he was fourteen. After his time in the army, he went to England to work, then immigrated to Canada where we met.

The climate in Scotland was freezing. The cold seeped into your bones. We slept under a mountain of blankets to keep warm and could hardly move.

"God," I said to Ben, "Is it always this cold; does anyone have central heating?"

He laughed, "You are spoiled, just put on more clothes."

I loved the historical and architectural buildings built so many years go. Ben's grandparents were born in Ireland. We flew to Ireland for a few days and I fell in love with Dublin. Its cobblestone streets, quaint restaurants and pubs and its magnificent churches were sights to behold. We stayed at the Gresham Hotel that was located in the center of the city. The hotel had such style and grace. The people were wonderful and friendly. We seemed to be a world away from our little pub in Chicago.

Having never been to Europe, I soaked up the wonderful scenery. Scotland is well known for its fine wool. Ben wanted to bring back sweaters, one for Chuck and also for others. Chuck was thrilled with his gift and seemed astounded that we thought of him.

For this trip I had two regrets, first that our Benny would not be with us and second, Ben's mother was gone. I swept the unhappy thoughts from my mind.

The girls stayed with my mother and Blanche for the first week. They could assist them in how to rent rooms and do the jobs associated with the motel. During our second week, the girls would fly to Scotland where we would spend time as a family. I would return home by plane with the four younger kids and the girls would travel home on the ship with their father.

I loved Scotland. It was cold, but the people were warm. The countryside was beautiful. It reminded me of my home in Canada. We traveled to the highlands where the scenery was breathtaking. It was such an innocent country and there were no guns. There was crime, but not on the same scale as the United States. Scotland was a small country with only a few large cities and many smaller ones. Its economy was on an upswing. One could see an enormous amount of construction going on. I felt safe. It had never occurred to me to move from the States. While on vacation, we looked at hotels and pubs that were for sale. We took note of a few of them, each one appearing busier that the next one. The pubs were being snapped up quickly. It was a thought.

The sale of Bob's motel was quick. It was too soon for the girls, who were not prepared to move. It took several months to close the transaction, giving them time to adjust to a new way of life.

CHAPTER 56: POINT OF NO RETURN

We discussed moving to Scotland at length. We thought that for the well being of the children and our own sanity it might be a good idea for the short term. This saga was never going to end. I had become increasingly nervous and jumpy. Every little thing would upset me. Ben encouraged me to take several trips back on my own to see what I thought about the idea. The fear I felt for my children's safety consumed me. I was not sleeping well and was always on edge.

One hotel in particular caught my attention, located in the city of Ayr and not in the countryside. I did not want the children to be isolated. I felt good about the move. Ben's father was elderly and would enjoy having us home.

Ben would have preferred not to move. His friend became head of the bricklayer union. He would always be guaranteed a job.

He also enjoyed the nightlife in this town, but knew his priorities. It was not his first choice, but for the sake of the children and me he knew it was necessary. In time, he did enjoy living back in Scotland. The hotel once again gave him a stage. We had the public bar, a lounge bar and with his skills he built a hall we named the "Americana." The hall held functions, dances and sing songs. It was not too long before he felt at home.

It was difficult saying goodbye to our son. I lingered at the cemetery for a long time, promising him we would come back. I knew he understood. Our thoughts were that we could not defend ourselves and keep our children safe. The Syndicate was too powerful and the law was too corrupt. Who could we trust? There was no alternative; we said goodbye to friends and family.

SCOTLAND, U.K.

SCOTLAND, U.K.

CHAPTER 57: SHOTGUN BLAST

Several days before I was about to embark on our new venture, I was listening to the news on television. Unexpectedly, I heard Sam's name mentioned. It was a news flash. I turned up the volume and stopped to listen. Sam had been gunned down in his garage at his home. Evidently the killer waited until he knew no one else was home.

A shotgun blast severed off his arm and a second shot hit him in the chest. The television station flashed a photo of him lying on the garage floor in pools of blood. It was rumored that Sam hated shotguns. The next day, the front page of every newspaper carried the story and picture. My only thought was, "Sam, I hope you rot in hell."

The newspaper played up the story of a true gangland assassination. There were no clues or witnesses. My first thought was that Chuck was responsible and I still believe that to this day. He knew the house well and was familiar with the family's habits. He also knew Sam hated shotguns. There are some articles and stories that Tony Spilotro and Sam's brother, Mario, killed Sam. Tony was also a collector and hitman. These men, including Chuck, were charged with the murder of Leo Foreman. Tony and Mario were first to go on trial and could not take any chances. It was common knowledge that Sam caused too many waves in the courts. If they got rid of Sam, there was a possibility they could go free. The trial was held on April 3, 1973 and Mario was convicted; I believe Tony was acquitted for the murder of Leo Foreman.

No one was held accountable for Sam's murder. The list of suspects was endless with too many names to count. He was ruthless; his reputation for violence and erratic behavior preceded itself, the unwanted publicity he attracted was a constant embarrassment. To best describe him, he was crazy and many people wanted him dead.

Very few people attended his funeral; most would not want to be seen. I could hardly wait to tell Ben, who was already in Scotland.

It was the end of a chapter in our life. In the spring of 1973, we moved to Scotland, a new beginning for us. The older children were apprehensive. They had friends here and Scotland was far away.

Before leaving I called Lieutenant Horner and asked him to stop by the motel. I handed him the gun. I said, "I don't think I will need this where we are going. I only used it once and that was enough." He smiled, took the gun and hugged me.

We never knew what caused the fire at our tavern. Was it an accident? Was it arson? Was it murder? There were no answers and officially the case was closed. Fires start somewhere. It will always leave doubt in my mind as to what really happened. We seemed to be the only ones that wanted answers. To me, this case will always remain open. Maybe one day the truth will prevail. They may not have been able to connect Chuck and Sam, but in my heart I knew they had a lot to do with the fire. Sam was a desperate man and Chuck was as guilty as he was.

May have tried earlier

Killers waited till hood was alone

By Ronald Yates
and Steven Pratt

Sam De Stefano

SAM De Stefano's West Side home was probably staked out for weeks before his gangland-style killing Saturday, homicide investigators believe.

"He had a bottomless pit of enemies who would have walked years to get him," one police man said. "It looks like they waited until he was alone to hit him."

De Stefano's bodyguard, Joseph Vallente, had left the mobster's West Side home at 1356 N. Sayre Av. about 9:40 a.m. san De Stefano's wife, Anita, police said. Vallente had driven her to visit her mother. De Stefano was found dead about 11:15 a.m. His body was sprawled on the garage floor with multiple shotgun wounds in the chest and left arm.

According to Shakespeare District homicide investigators, a coroner's autopsy revealed that De Stefano was suffering from acute malnutrition.

POLICE theorized that the killers of the slant-eyed man drove to the driveway may have even gone the short distance the killing earlier this month.

On April 1, De Stefano's home was reported burglarized by someone who not only used a hacksaw to gain entrance but also had a key to De Stefano's elaborate burglar alarm system and knew exactly where the system's secret cutoff ...

attempting to track down a ... gold and white car that ... least two neighbors had seen parked near De Stefano's home just before the shooting.

"This killing could take months and months to solve. The guy had so many enemies that you could search from now till doomsday for the killer," an investigator said.

De Stefano's long career in the Chicago mob had made him a magnet for enemies.

EVEN OTHER mobsters called him an animal, a sadist, and the Marquis de Sade of the mob. By thinking with his enemies were legend.

He once tied a naked man to a red hot radiator and on another occasion ordered that one enemy be hung on a meat hook.

He was indicted last August for the brutal 1963 slaying of Leo Foreman, a one-time racketeer. His trial was to have begun May 30. Also scheduled for a separate trial are De Stefano's brother Mario, 57, and Anthony Spilotro, 36, former triggerman for the late mob chief Felix (Milwaukee Phil) Alderisio.

According to a federal undercover informant, who had led a falling out with his confederates, and these men even a hint that he may have turned state's evidence to get a lighter sentence.

DE STEFANO'S emergence on the Chicago mob scene be-

real Penitentiary, where he was released, he met two imprisoned gangsters, Paul (the Waiter) Ricca and Louis Campagna.

WHEN HE was released, he went on the city payroll as a laborer. He passed the civil service examination for garbage dump foreman in 1948 and lied on his application about his prison record.

In 1952 the city corporation counsel ruled that the city could fire civil service charges against De Stefano for falsifying his job application. No charges were ever filed against him, and he was on the city payroll for a while.

In 1955, De Stefano was accused of killing his own brother, Michael, another city pavement. Underworld informants said he had stabbed his brother with a knife and then washed the body with soap and water to cleanse his soul. Michael was a dope addict.

In 1963 the body of Leo Foreman was found in the trunk of a car at 1350 W. Chicago Av. The 42-year-old reputed loan shark bore 14 bullet wounds, stabbed, and shot.

DE STEFANO was suspected but nothing could be proved. Evidence technicians vacuumed Foreman's clothing and discovered several paint and wood chips embedded in the fabric. The chips were placed in a bottle, sealed, and put on a shelf.

Last year, Charles Crimaldi,

who described himself as a former collector of usurious loans and "hit man" for De Stefano, was granted immunity from prosecution for his testimony in the Foreman murder.

Crimaldi told a grand jury that De Stefano had lured Foreman, who owed him $1,000, to his Sayre Avenue home. When Foreman got there, he was met by Sam and Mario, who pulled their guns and drove him to the Mario's home at 1304 S. Cicero Av., Cicero, Crimaldi said.

"There he was beaten by Sam De Stefano with a baseball bat, shot, and stabbed. Foreman lay bleeding and dying, he pleaded with De Stefano to spare him. Crimaldi said, but Sam answered, "I told you I'd get you."

IN 1972 Mario said he had once exactly what investigators had been waiting for since 1963. They obtained warrants, entered the home, and went over the floor with their scrap.

Paint and wood chips as well as blood specks, and those that had been from Foreman's body and kept nine years in the sealed bottle. Based on that evidence and Crimaldi's testimony, indictments were returned against De Stefano, his brother, and Spilotro.

According to one source, De Stefano's trial would have cost the taxpayers of Cook County at least $15,000.

223

Norma McCluskie

Many wanted DeStefano dead

SAM DeSTEFANO

IF POLICE INVESTIGATORS fail to find the killer of crime syndicate juice loan shark Sam DeStefano, it won't be because they have no suspects.

Their list of suspects, in fact, is long enough to rival the procession of mourners past the slain gangster's bier.

DeStefano, 64, was found shotgunned to death Saturday in the garage of his spacious ranch style home at 1656 N. Sayre Av. In true gangland fashion, his slayer(s) left few clues and saw to it there were no witnesses. The without clues, police are not without motives.

DeSTEFANO, WHO amassed a fortune in the juice loan racket, was one of the most successful of mobsters, but not one of the most trusted. His reputation for violent and erratic behavior and the unwanted publicity it attracted were a constant sources of irritation and embarrassment to his cohorts.

Their resentment reached a peak recently, according to informed sources, when De-Stefano insisted on having a government witness against him assassinated.

DeStefano, his brother Mario, and syndicate terrorist Anthony Spilotro, now a boutique owner in Las Vegas, Nev., are accused of the 1963 murder of loan shark Leo Foreman, who reportedly owed DeStefano $3,000.

DeStefano, who often acted as his own lawyer, was out on bond and was to go to trial in Criminal Court May 30. The others were to be prosecuted separately.

THE STATE'S KEY witness in the prosecution is mob informer Charles Crimaldi, who is being held in protective custody under tight security.

Informed sources said the heat from law enforcement agencies generated by the impending trial already had singed the nerves of crime syndicate leaders, when DeStefano insisted that they have Crimaldi killed. He threatened to "blow the whistle" on his colleagues if they failed to honor his request.

There was a time when the "wild man" of Chicago gangland might have gotten away with such an outrageous request. B: was before Oct. 11, 1972, when DeSte powerful patron, Paul [The Waiter] died at the of 74.

RICCA, THE "GODFATHER" of the cago crime family and DeStefano had close friends since 1947, when they in inmates in the Federal Penitentia Leavenworth, Kas., where DeStefano doing a one-year sentence for selling co teit sugar ration stamps.

His talkativeness and wild antics kep in and out of the news and under the of the police. One of his most remem escapades came in 1964, when he delt himself in Circuit Court on a charg illegal voting.

Claiming to be ill, he had himself c: into courtroom on a stretcher and te megaphone to amplify his weakened

The act drew guffaws from his audien the courtroom, but out in the neighborl where the crime syndicate operates its : ness, there were some who weren't laugh

224

Suntimes Two   Midwest   Travel

CLOUDY
Showers likely Sunday. High near 70.
Details on Page 121

CHICAGO SUNDAY
Sun-Times

Sunday, April 15, 1973

FINAL

40c

Mobster DeStefano found shot to death

By Paul Galloway

Mobster Sam DeStefano, 64, was found shot Saturday in the garage of his home by ... police who went there to ... burglary of his

... known how many times DeStefano had been shot but that [one arm was badly mangled."

He said the DeStefanos had reported a burglary of their home on April 5 and that the burglary investigators had gone to the yellow brick house to talk to the couple about the break-in.

There was speculation that DeStefano was ... Fitzgerald said neighbors ... shots had ... about 10 ...

... of an unusually garrulous crime figure. DeStefano was often flamboyant in a bizarre way and his life was linked with violence.

Identified as a loan shark boss before the U.S. Senate Rackets Committee in 1963, DeStefano and served prison terms for bank robbery, black marketing, rape and perjury.

He also had been convicted of assault with a deadly weapon, contempt of court and judge-raping.

His most recent conviction came in March ... he was sentenced to 3½ years in ... ... for threatening ...

... ernment witness in a narcotics trial. The U.S. District Court conviction was upheld in February by the U.S. Court of Appeals.

DeStefano also was indicted by a county grand jury of the 1963 murder of Leo Foreman, whose mutilated body was found in the trunk of his car in November, 1963.

DeStefano's body remained at the murder scene at mid-day as police investigators searched the house. The body lay uncovered where it was found. DeStefano was wearing gray sportswear over a white shirt and dark ...

225

Tribune, Tuesday, April 17, 1973   Section 1A   13

Few attend rites for De Stefano

By William Mullen

AFTER YEARS of being excluded from most of the underworld's prime social gatherings—the funerals—Sam De Stefano, attended one yesterday.

The trouble was, it was his own.

To add insult to, injury, it was not a traditional mobland extravaganza usually accorded to the brighter lights who ascend to the syndicate's pantheon of fallen family members.

For Sam, the syndicate provided only a quick and simple ceremony at the Queen of Heaven Cemetery Chapel and a 10-car caravan to his family burial spot at the Mt. Carmel Cemetery in Hillside.

The 64-year-old juice loan racketeer, slain in his garage Saturday, wouldn't have liked that had he been around, for he surely thought of himself as one of the bigger luminaries in Chicago organized crime.

own funeral amplified what police had known for years. De Stefano, indeed, was one of the most hated mobsters around, despised by his victims and associates alike.

The depth of contempt in which he was held by all who knew him has presented a monumental problem to police trying to solve his murder.

Practically everybody who ever had contact with him is being regarded as a suspect.

His assassination by shotgun could have been ordered by the syndicate's ruling echelon who feared he might become overly talkative in a murder trial pending against him next month.

The hushed-up, rushed-up services for DeStefano, typical for underworld members who have fallen out of favor, were monitored by members of the Chicago police organized crime unit and the Federal Bureau of Investigation.

They were watching to see if any of the tears shed over Sam

CHAPTER 58: EXPLOITATION

It was several years later when friends sent us several newspaper articles relating to Chuck Crimaldi. After Sam's death, little was written, plus we were out of the country.

What I am about to write is what I can remember about the articles written in the Chicago Tribune. The newspaper reporter, Bob Wiedrich, had an exclusive interview with Chuck between the dates of July 3, 1973 and July 10, 1973. The articles described many of the workings of the Syndicate and contained stories and descriptions of Chuck's twenty-year criminal career leading to him becoming a hitman. In this series of accounts he gives his version of his life and his involvement in the Syndicate. The articles suggested to me, as far as I could understand, that Chuck was Sam's errand boy. How much is hype fabrication, or the truth, you be the judge.

It was a coincidence that at the same time as these articles appeared, a customer gave us a book. He said, "Your name is in this book, want to read it?" The book *Hit Man* was written by Crimaldi. The story was similar to the newspaper accounts, only he elaborated on his importance and self worth. He spoke with pride and enjoyed bragging about his accomplishments. He was a hitman.

In the book it appeared that in order to protect himself, many of the dates and times were changed. The story focused on how he began his career as a gangster, his involvement with the Syndicate and the hits he did for Sam. The book contained no sign of remorse, only arrogance and he was flippant about his deeds.

Chuck portrayed himself as a killer who killed for all the right reasons. He justified himself as a man who only killed people who deserved to die. He liked to play God. Who was he to make judgments on anyone? He claimed he cared about people and defends everything he is guilty of. Who was Chuck? He was nobody. He liked to believe he was important, but Sam used him for his own indulgences. He thought he was a big man with a baseball bat and a gun.

Why we were in his book baffles me. A story should be truthful and the chapter on Ben's Place was far from honest. Therefore, one would have to question the accuracy of the rest of his book and the account of his life. Chuck knew the facts since he was there, but chose to ignore them. He knew exactly how the robbery occurred and the incidents that followed, as I have described in the first chapters of this book. Of course, the truth would incriminate him and make him look stupid. This is not the image he wanted to portray. The Feds used him for their own purpose and may have bought his story, but I did not. I threw the book away and assured our customer it probably was someone with the same names as us, just a coincidence. In the newspaper articles and his book these were some of the stories that he disclosed and the truth of them is questionable.

According to Chuck, Sam was trying to conduct his business from within the prison walls. His wife Anita and Chuck did not agree on how the business should be run. It seemed Anita wanted to quit the loan business. She refused to give Chuck the funds for new loans. She blamed Chuck for the failure of loans and collections. Sam also blamed Chuck because of the information Anita gave him. Chuck had not been allowed to visit Sam in the jail to explain what was happening.

Somehow Sam managed to manipulate the officials into believing he was ill. He was admitted into a hospital where he stayed in a private room for a month. Because visitors were allowed, Chuck finally was able to visit and try to explain the disagreement he was having with Anita. Sam indicated he would take care of the situation.

He instructed Chuck on numerous hits he wanted on several men. "When I am returned to the prison, I'll give you a list of who I want whacked. I will give it to Anita and I don't care how you do it." Chuck agreed.

Sam was livid with the Circuit Court Judge, Nathan Cohen, who had given him the three to five-year sentence for our case—conspiring to commit perjury. And he also was irritated with his criminal attorney, Julius Echeles, who lost the case defending him. There were several other men Sam wanted taken care of, but these were his priorities.

These hits were never carried out as the dispute between Chuck and Anita continued. She withheld the monies Chuck needed to make loans. He was losing his credibility when he could not deliver as promised to clients. As a consequence, Chuck quit his job. Anita was stunned. He claimed he informed the people who owed Sam money that he no longer collected for Sam. They did not have to pay him back as he was in prison. The other reason he gave for splitting from Sam was that Sam had indicated he was going into the drug trade. Because of his brother Tony, this was a sore spot. Chuck was a marked man and from within the prison walls, Sam hired a hitman to take care of a hitman.

Where money was concerned, Sam hated to lose. This was apparent in the way he dealt with Leo Foreman, a real estate agent who also was a collector. He did collections for Sam for about three years. Sam, convinced he was dishonest, despised him to the point that it became an obsession. If he thought anyone was cheating him, he went to great lengths to hunt them down. The sum of money, large or small, was not the object. To him it was the principal. Anyone who thought to use his money to further their own pleasure or fortunes paid a price.

Foreman believed he was forgiven and was invited by Mario to his house. He was lured into the basement where he was struck with a baseball bat, shot and stabbed as he begged for his life. Several days later, he bled to death. Chuck, Sam and Mario and another hitman, Tony Spilotro, were involved in this brutal physical attack. They had taunted him for days, enjoying his anguish; this was a game to them. The police later found his body in the trunk of his car.

De Stefano Convicted in Threat Case

BY ROBERT DAVIS

Sam De Stefano, 63, reputed crime syndicate figure, and an associate, Edward Speice, 46, were found guilty by a Federal District Court jury yesterday of threatening a witness during a federal narcotics trial last month.

Judge Richard B. Austin said he would sentence both men at 10 a. m. today. He also said he would rule on whether the two men should be allowed to remain free on bond pending their expected appeals.

James R. Thompson, United States attorney who handled the prosecution of the case, recommended that no appeal bond be set. He also asked that De Stefano be sentenced to a maximum term of five years and levied a $5,000 fine. He recommended a three-year jail sentence and a $3,000 fine for Speice, who lives at 2650 N. Harlem Av., Elmwood Park.

Victim Not Called

Both men were accused of threatening Charles Crimaldi, a government witness during the narcotics trial of Anthony Esposito, 35. Crimaldi was not called as a witness during the De Stefano trial over the strong objections of Frank Oliver, Speice's attorney, and De Stefano, who acted as his own lawyer.

After the verdict was returned, Judge Austin told the jury that Crimaldi was not produced as a witness because ernment could not protect members of the Kennedy family, it could not protect him.

Thanks the Jury

As the jury was leaving the courtroom, De Stefano stood up and said in a soft voice, "I wish to thank you for doing your duty as you saw it. Thank you all."

Altho De Stefano had acted as his own lawyer during the often frantic trial, he said after the verdicts that he immediately would hire Julius Echeles to act as his lawyer on the appeal.

The jury reached a verdict after about 10 hours of deliberations. As it deliberated, a major witness for De Stefano was named in a perjury complaint for telling the jury the government planned to frame De Stefano.

"Frame Plot" Told

Louis Tragas, 42, of 3757 N. Monticello Av., had testified that he overheard a federal agent and Crimaldi discuss the frame of De Stefano during the Esposito trial.

Yesterday's action marked the end of a strange case which took only nine days from the indictment to the verdict.

De Stefano and Speice were indicted on March 7 and they were arraigned the next day when they demanded an immediate trail. The trial began

Charles Siragusa of the Illinois Crime Commission and an FBI agent had convinced Charles Crimaldi to furnish intelligence information about the loan shark business and the drug trade. They also wanted Chuck to provide specifics on the slaying of Leo Foreman at Mario DeStefano's trial. Chuck became a government special agent for his testimony and received immunity from his involvement in the murder of Leo Foreman. He was the star witness in the conviction of Mario DeStefano.

Chuck also was to testify against Sam during the federal narcotics case against Anthony Esposito. This trial was scheduled for February 22, 1972. He would not testify in person because he was afraid of Sam. He claimed that if the United State's government could not protect the Kennedy family, it certainly could not protect him. His testimony was on a tape-recorded telephone conversation, which was played in the presence of the jury. The case was about a Louis Tragus who had testified that he overheard a federal agent and Chuck Crimaldi discussing a way to frame DeStefano throughout the Esposito trail. Sam was convicted of threatening to murder a government witness in the Esposito trail. Chuck was held in protective custody under tight security. He was the state's key witness for the prosecution.

Chuck became a government informant and received immunity and a new identity sometime in 1968 or 1969. The immunity would only apply to the Foreman case. In his stories, he does not disclose how many people he killed because murder has no statute of limitations. He began working for one of Sam's rivals when the FBI approached him. According to some accounts, he was giving out information before he became a government agent. This was probably why he was never brought to trial on our case. The Outfit put out a $50,000 contract for information about his whereabouts.

It was interesting how he had converted from a criminal to a witness for the prosecution assisting the State's Attorney's Office, giving evidence against Sam. According to news reports, he also took the stand in criminal court, confessing to his involvement as a hired hitman.

Sam was out on bond, but after all his appeals were exhausted, he went to prison sometime in 1969. I believe he served his time and was back on the streets in 1971. Chuck had to be concerned that Sam was out of prison as a threat to his life was imminent. In April 1973, Sam was murdered before he was brought to trial in the Foreman case. His trial had been scheduled separate from the others involved.

I find it ironic and do not understand why we reward people for bad behavior in order to convict someone else. Chuck suddenly became the good guy, claiming he gave up his life of crime. Here was a guy who murdered people for money. A killer in this profession for over twenty years, he must have killed countless people.

My biggest disappointment was Charles Siragusa, who I thought put his job before people. We were victims and I felt he used Chuck for information. Chuck turned State's evidence to save himself, even though he cites other reasons, such as the drug trade. He also claims he still takes part in crimes because he loves the power and the prestige. Regardless of what Crimaldi had done, he received a new lease on life. He remarried and received protection and a second chance. My son lost his life because of people like him. I felt we were denied the justice our son deserved. The authorities showed no compassion for the injured people whose lives were shattered when a family member was murdered or maimed for life because of him.

Ben said, "Don't be bitter, Norma, it will ruin your life. We need to move on." He was right, but being right did not change things. I knew I would move on. It had to be in my own time and on my own terms. I could not sweep everything under the carpet. I was not ready to forgive and forget. I was not like Ben; he did not want to see faults in people, only good things. This was the right way, except it was too soon for me.

CHAPTER 59: CONCLUSIONS

Living abroad was a different kind of experience. People were friendly in the small town. Pubs were run in the same manner as in the States, except there were no guns. Most men only had fistfights that could also be dangerous. What I loved most was that the children had the freedom to play freely. There was no anxiety of terrible things happening to them. It was a childhood similar to ours.

We lived abroad for several years, and then decided to return to the U.S.A. in 1980. The children deserved the good things that their country offered. Our children are grown, married and have children of their own. We have many grandchildren and great-grandchildren.

DIANE, JAMIE, SEAN

BRAEHEAD HOTEL, AYR, SCOTLAND, U.K

CHAPTER 60: MEMORIES

We return to Chicago as often as we can. We drive past Albany Avenue and our thoughts return to that time long ago. We choke back the tears.

The neighborhood has changed, but we still see it as it was. The pub is a dwelling house now. We visit our son at Saint Joseph's cemetery in Baby Land. We say a prayer, but the sadness is still there. We visualize him as he was and wonder what he could have been. Someday we may have the answers we crave. Our children now visit his grave a lot more than we do, since we do not travel much anymore. Hopefully our grandchildren and our great-grandchildren will take up this same practice so he is never forgotten. His influence in each of our lives has made a difference. He is our guardian angel.

A FOOTNOTE

In 2007, our sons, a daughter and a grandson arranged a trip to Chicago for us. Ben and I believed this would be our last trip. Our visit to the cemetery was difficult for Ben as he climbed that short hill. The dancing feet were gone, but his spirit was alive and well. I stood for a while at Benny's gravesite as we planted our flowers and prayed silently. I still felt the urge to tear up the ground; just to hold him once more. Benny never had the chance to reach his dreams. I often wondered if his existence was more rewarding than our own. After all he is one of the children of God. He was privileged, his passage was short, but his accomplishments were great.

I look at my children and grand children, how wonderful they turned out with his guidance. He was always there for the good times, the bad times and us. His input into our lives spoke volumes. Thanks, Son, for being with me every step of the way. We all adore you and there is something of you in all of us. It has been a long journey.

My children, now adults, walked away so I could spend time with him. I promised him we would see him soon. I am sure he smiled. He spirit is always in our thoughts and in our hearts. The angel on his headstone reminded me of the angels from so long ago.

We strolled down memory lane visiting Albany Avenue, which was now a dwelling house. How nice it looked with its well-kept grass and beautiful, colorful flowers everywhere. The bright red fire hydrant caught my eye and I wondered if it worked now. The new green awnings trimmed in white on the windows and above the doors looked nice. The front door and side door had been altered.

The cracks in the sidewalks had been repaired and the building had been painted a bright red color giving it an appearance of newness.

The windows seemed different, the facade of a home rather than a pub. At the back of the building, there stood a new white painted porch. I could not help but remember Benny hanging out one of those windows the day before he died. Ben had scolded, "You were just protecting him."

I was pleased that the building was so well preserved. There was a new garage and the tenants kept the place nice and orderly. The streets and alley appeared much narrower than I remembered. The empty lot had a colorful gazebo on it.

The building appeared smaller; outside of that it had not changed very much. An air conditioner was hanging out the window of the kitchen the same way as when we lived there.

How many times I had stood at that window, to watch the children play or see a customer walking towards the pub. Sometimes they looked up and we would wave to each other.

Once the children thought they saw Santa and his sleigh out that window. I remember how excited they were. They said, "Mommy, Santa is going to land on our roof." I smiled at them, they were so innocent. "Look, look," they shouted, "Can you see him." "Yes," I replied, "I can see him, but he will not come until you are all asleep." With those words they scurried to their beds.

ALBANY AVENUE, CHICAGO, ILL.

BEN'S PLACE, ALBANY AVE, CHICAGO, ILL

ALBANY AVENUE, CHICAGO, ILL

I stood and stared at the front of the building and could visualize Ben putting the children and me out that window. They appeared to be the same windows and yet they seemed so narrow, it was a wonder we fit through them.

The smoke billowed through the windows and I could feel the horror and smell the smoke. My body shuddered as I imagined the customers standing on the sidewalk, shouting under our bedroom window. How many times had I looked out that window? The terror I felt on that fatal night as the rock came sailing through it? I closed my eyes and could hear the voices shouting. "Get out, get out, the building is on fire."

The sign was gone; a light fixture in its place. I watched Ben drop from the sign before he fell to the ground running. People were running everywhere and I remember how I rejoiced when I heard the sirens and saw the fire trucks, only to be disappointed. It was a traumatic night, one I will never forget.

The street seemed narrow now; the factory across the street appeared closer to the pub. The building, also painted a bright red color, looked new. The weeds were gone, there were no papers flying around. It was difficult to believe it was the same factory that stood there so many years ago. The neighborhood was quiet, almost like a ghost town. Where did all the excitement and life go that was here so long ago?

CRIBEAN AND SEXTON FACTORY, ALBANY AVE,

All five pubs were gone. The 700 Club had been torn down and an apartment building stood in its place. Many of the homes were replaced with factories. The street appeared empty and lonely.

The factory was different then. There was so much activity. I could still hear the men shouting greetings to each other as they went to work. They were cheerful as they descended upon the pub for lunch and a drink. There were the children playing on the street, riding their bikes. I smiled as I stood at that window watching them. The neighborhood was alive.

We drove around the area and Trisha could visualize her childhood. I hope it brought her some closure. We could not find Saint Mathew's Church or School. We asked, but no one had heard of it. Marty was a baby and Sean was not born yet. All the children felt our sorrow. I believe they became better people because of him. It was a long time ago; there are only memories, now. Time changes everything. I closed my eyes. I could see the tavern, alive and vibrant, a busy neighborhood full of population, and now it was quiet. I whispered a silent goodbye as we drove away.

There is a time to be born, a time to live, and a time to die. It is what we do with our time to live that's important. We felt we made the right decision.

About the Author

Norma and Bernard McCluskie moved to Florida in 1980. After Norma retired in 2006 at the age of 72, she began to seriously work on *A Decade of Fear,* a non-fiction book that she had thought about writing for many years. Norma and Bernard have been married over 50 years and enjoy their retirement along with the 6 children, 16 grandchildren, and 6 great-grandchildren.

Made in the USA
Columbia, SC
28 January 2020